# The Divine Dynamic

*Exploring the Relationships between Humans,
Earth, and the Creative Power of the Universe*

*John Surette, SJ*

**acta**
PUBLICATIONS

**THE DIVINE DYNAMIC**
**Exploring the Relationships between Humans, Earth,**
**and the Creative Power of the Universe**
by John Surette, SJ

Edited by Gregory F. Augustine Pierce
Cover by Tom A. Wright
Cover Art, "Bright Wings, Beams of Love," by Mary Southard, CSJ,
    courtesy of Ministry of the Arts, Lagrange, Illinois
Text design and typesetting by Patricia A. Lynch

Published by ACTA Publications, 4848 N. Clark Street,
Chicago, IL 60640, (800) 397-2282, www.actapublications.com

Library of Congress Catalog number: 2010933000
ISBN: 978-0-87946-433-2
Printed in the United States of America by Versa Press
Year 20 19 18 17 16 15 14 13 12 11 10
Printing 15 14 13 12 11 10 9 8 7 6 5 4 3 2 First

♻ Text printed on 30% post-consumer recycled paper

# Contents

# Dedication

*To Thomas Berry*
*Mentor Inspiration Friend*

☙

# PROLOGUE

During my early adolescent years I was gifted with some powerful religious experiences in the context of the natural world. While sitting around campfires and staring into that part of the flame that has no boundaries and while looking up at the stars at night and expecting them to speak to me out of their silence, I felt a oneness with the cosmos. I felt part of a much larger reality and at home within that immensity. I experienced wonder, amazement, and even felt loved. Looking back I now know that the whole arrow of my life was being revealed to me in those experiences.

Then I went to the university and majored in chemistry. I absorbed much of what mechanistic science had to teach me. I learned that matter is just stuff and that it has no spiritual dimension, no voice, no within, and carries no mystery. I also studied biology and learned about evolution, dabbled in geology, and became aware of the fantastic ages of the rocks. However, I didn't make any connections between these scientific facts and the meaning of my life. How far I had drifted from my early adolescent experiences.

After several years studying philosophy and theology I found myself working in the Caribbean islands and territories. There I was caught up in the pathos of the human situation. Although surrounded by so much natural beauty, I couldn't see much beyond human pain and suffering and the unjust structures that kept the people oppressed.

I was well into my fifties when my worldview began to change. Like the biblical Noah, I found myself deposited on a new shore. At times I was scared and confused, and at other times excited and energized. I was undergoing what is popularly known as a paradigm shift. I was living within a new world view and therefore within a new understanding and experience of myself.

Cultural historian Thomas Berry (1914-2009) became my mentor at that time. I attended a lecture that he gave in 1989. I had always been fascinated with the relationship of the Divine and the human, so when Thomas started to speak about the Divine-human relationship my antennae extended to their maximum. For most of my years as a priest, I had been involved in human problems and the challenges of social justice, so when Thomas spoke about the human-human relationship I felt comfortable and much at home. Then he began to speak about the Earth-human relationship. Memories of my early adolescent experiences stirred in my soul. I was eager to learn more.

That *more* came when he wove the three relationships together. I forget his exact words but they went somewhat like this: Continued progress in the Divine-human relationship and continued progress in the human-human relationship, now for the first time ever, depends upon progress in the Earth-human relationship. Upon hearing these words, from deep inside of me, emerged this response: Yes! This is true! At that very moment I knew that for the rest of my life I would focus on the Earth-human relationship, knowing that in doing so I would continue to be working on the human-human and the Divine-human.

This was my primary motivation as I wrote this book. It is my hope that as you read these pages you will begin to understand and experience the Divine-human relationship, the human-human relationship, and the Earth-human relationship that together form one sacred relationship in your one sacred life.

John Surette, SJ
Planet Earth
The Universe
Year 13,700,000,000

# I

# THE PROMISE OF MORE

*Billions of years before our own appearance in evolution*
*it was already seeded with promise.*
*John Haught*

~~

No matter where we focus our attention in the 13.7 billion year unfolding of the Universe, we find the promise of *more*. We find it at the beginning, throughout history, and also in our present moment.

In its original flaring forth the Universe expressed itself as a plasma of charged particles and energy. The temperature of the plasma was in the order of a thousand million degrees centigrade. That primordial furnace contained the promise of atoms. And so it happened, after less than a million years, the plasma cooled and the particles were able to come together and form atoms of hydrogen and helium. Very quickly the Universe took the form of galactic clouds of these gases. These galaxies, billions of them, foamed into existence.

The galaxies held the promise of stars. And so it happened, that due to the attracting force of gravity, the molecules of hydrogen and helium were drawn together where they ignited and the primal stars burst into being. These stars, millions of them in each galaxy, lit up the Universe like a cosmic Christmas tree.

One of the stars contained the promise of our solar system. And so it happened, several billion years ago, that a star (recently named "Tiamat") grew old, swelled, and exploded with the brilliance of a billion stars, scattering its dust into space. It was a supernova! Again the uniting force of gravity was at work. Over time the dust from that star was drawn together, where it ignited and gave birth to many stars, including the one we call the Sun. It was from the scraps of that birth that our beautiful planet Earth was born.

The early Earth contained the promise of life. And so it happened, some four billion years ago, that conditions were such that life was able to emerge within Earth's ocean in the form of tiny one-celled creatures. For millions of years they cleaned the waters, added oxygen to the atmosphere, and prepared the way for every different and complex form of life that was to follow. Among those who followed were we humans, that most creative and unpredictable of creatures.

**The *more* that the Universe promises points to a Mystery that is full of surprises and delights in change and adventure.**

The promise of *more* was embedded in humankind. And so it happened over the past 200,000 years that we humans moved from being hunter-gatherers to becoming village and then city dwellers. We dared to dream dreams and see visions. We created language and art, literature and poetry, philosophy and theology, science and technology, and in modern times through our science we have taken into ourselves the very powers of the Universe itself.

The evolving Universe is essentially promise. Its creative energy carries this great promise of abundance, of fulfillment, of *more*. The *more* turns out to be galaxies, stars, planets, Earth, life—including all of us reading these words at this very moment, with all that moves deeply within us.

The *more* of the Universe is often not predictable or even imaginable. A charged particle in the primordial plasma could not have foretold atoms of hydrogen and helium. Those atoms could not have imagined stars and galaxies. Tiamat could not have predicted our beautiful planet Earth, and Earth's early life forms could not have forecast the human adventure. In recent times, for example, who among us could have predicted the disintegration of the Soviet Union or the collapse of Apartheid in South Africa or the emergence within Maoist China of a capitalist economy?

The *more* that the Universe promises often turns out to be a total surprise and as such points to Ultimate Mystery that is *more* than we can ever imagine. It points to a Mystery that is full of surprises and delights in change and adventure. Such a Universe provides the cosmic basis for the hope of fulfillment that resides at the core of the great religions and in the hearts of all peoples. This hope invites us into our future and moves us into action in the present moment.

The promise of *more* also provides us with the basis for an ecological ethic. It nurtures within us humans an intensified sense of responsibility for Earth, within which such promise is embedded. It fosters an ecological justice, a justice that is sensitive to all creatures that carry within themselves the evolutionary Divine Dynamic. It makes evident to us that to contribute to the diminishment of Earth and its human community is to despair of the promise and of the Maker of the promise.

Many look at our twenty-first century world, with its ever-growing problems and perceive an historical process leading to chaos. Experiencing a lessening of their optimism for the future, such people yearn for the "good old days." Others look at the same radical changes that are taking place in our world and perceive the resulting chaos as a necessary condition for the emergence of the something *more* that has been promised from the beginning. These are the people who will lead us into our future as a human community. They are the ones who experience the Divine Dynamic as a source of potential energy, an energy for moving forward and dealing creatively with the challenges and invitations of our time, an energy for the enhancement of our human adventure.

As citizens of the Universe we know that this Dynamic plays out in our individual human lives. If the promise of *more* is carried by the whole cosmos, we know that the promise is available to us in our present moment. And so it does not surprise us that we are never satisfied and carry deep within ourselves an endless aching need.

Our hearts are restless, and when we experience this restlessness we are participating in the promise of *more* that pulsates throughout the Universe. The universal is present in the particular and the particular participates in the universal. The cosmic yearning for more and our individual yearning for more are one yearning. An evolving Universe encourages us to believe and to trust that there is always...*more*.

## Reflection ᴄᴏ Taking promises seriously

*They who have my commandments and keep them are those who love me; and those who love me will be loved by my Father, and I will love them and reveal myself to them. (John 14:21)*

Pay attention to these words from the Gospel of John. They contain a promise.

Our hopes are often based on a promise that has been made. What is distinctive of us Christians is our hope in the promise of Easter, of resurrection, of transformation—not just at the end of time but throughout all of time including our present time.

Consider the age of the Universe, an almost imaginable length of time, and that those of us living in this twenty-first century are members of that Universe. Such a long period of time carries the promise of the Divine commitment to and investment in the Universe. It carries the promise of God being profoundly faithful over deep time and therefore faithful in our present time. Because of this faithfulness we can have hope in the future.

Consider the promise made to Abraham and Sarah that they would have descendents as numerous as the grains of sand of the seashore. Because of that promise, in their old age the couple left behind all that was familiar and set out with hope into a new and unfamiliar land.

Consider the promise made to the Hebrew slaves in Egypt, the promise of a land flowing with milk and honey. Because of that promise, with a hope to offset their anxieties and fears, they set out on some forty years of wandering in the wilderness.

Consider each moment of dawn, as Earth turns toward its Sun. That turning carries the promise of the continuation and the newness of life. With such a promise we are able to enter into each new day with hope in its giftedness. Consider each moment of dusk, as Earth turns away from its Sun. The turning carries the promise that the darkness of night is not the final word. Because of that promise we can close our eyes in sleep, expecting to awake to the gift of a new day in the morning.

Consider each time a seed is planted. The very act of planting carries the promise that as a result of going down into the soil the seed will grow into the total surprise that is a new plant. So the seed is placed into the ground with the hope that it will yield plenty. Consider also the times when we have taken the risk of reaching out in love to another. This risk contains the promise of communion, of relatedness, and of intimacy.

Consider each time we pray for peace or work for justice in our world. The very act of praying or working carries the promise that the overwhelming brutality of what is happening within our human community need not be the final state of affairs. And so with hope we can continue with our praying and our working.

Consider all the ways in which we humans are diminishing and destroying planet Earth. We are tempted to despair over this pathological situation and wonder if anything can be done to reverse what is happening. Instead, we find the courage to hope for and imagine a better relationship between Earth and its human community. Our hoping for and imagining of this better relationship carries the promise of a new way forward.

All these experiences carry the hope of a more fully human life for all of us. Our hopes carry the promises of a better future, a future that is making its presence felt in our present moment.

## *Reflection ∽ The Promise Maker*

> *Then he said to Thomas, "Put your finger here and see my hands. Reach out your hand and put it in my side. Do not doubt, but believe." (John 20:27)*

It seems that believing came more easily in earlier times than it does now. It seems that it was easier for our parents and grandparents to believe than it is for us, and for us to believe than it is for our children. I am not certain of this, but generally speaking I suspect that it is true.

Why is it true? One answer is to be found in the degree of affluence that many of us in the developed world have achieved. Somehow all of our possessions prevent us from seeing with the eyes of faith. Somehow having so much stuff makes it more difficult to experience our dependence upon the Divine. Somehow having so many material things keeps us from experiencing the social and spiritual things. We are reminded of the Gospel teaching that it is more difficult for the rich person than it is for the poor person to enter the Kingdom of God. We are reminded of the often-repeated invitation of Jesus to those of us who have much that we should share what we have with others.

A second reason it is more difficult to believe in modern times has to do with the ever-increasing pace of change in all aspects of our lives. For example, prior to the Second Vatican Council (1962-1965) there was little change in our Church, and so the answers to the big and important questions we received when we were younger were to a large extent the same answers that were given when we were older. But now, many of the answers given when we were younger today sound quaint, somewhat out-of-date, inadequate, and not helpful in the light of our modern problems and challenges. In earlier times, when life was more static and involved less change, believing was easier. In our twenty-first century, when life is anything but static and unchanging, being persons of faith is something to which we need to give more attention, time, and energy.

A third reason that believing is more difficult today has to do with our diminished awareness of the Divine promises to us. The faith of Abraham and Sarah was founded on God's promise. The faith of the Israelites during their forty years of wandering in the desert was sustained by God's promise. The faith of Jesus and his disciples was steeped in the promise of the Reign of God, a world of justice, peace, and love. We Christians are part of that long line coming down from Abraham and Sarah through Jesus and his disciples. Accordingly, each of these promises is also made to us.

We once thought that the Universe was unchanging. Now we know that it has been unfolding for billions of years and that it carries the promise of change for billions of years to come. As citizens of that Universe and its Earth our lives also carry this same promise of change. And so we know that our lives and therefore our faith will continue to unfold and that new truths will be revealed to us as the years unfold.

The life of each of us, no matter what stage we are in, carries God's promise of something more. For Catholics, our Church, despite its slowness to be concerned about the fate of Earth and its clerical abuse scandal, carries God's promise that the gates of hell will not prevail against her. Our world, despite all of the violence and war, carries God's promise of becoming a city shining on the mountaintop. Our Earth, despite all its ecological diminishment and destruction, carries the Divine promise of greater abundance.

## Reflection ⌒ Dancing on the cutting edges

*Do not be afraid; from now on you will be catching people. (Luke 5:10)*

In this story from the Gospel of Luke, the apostle Peter is standing on the shore of Lake Gennesarth with his sandals off and his knees shaking out of fear as Jesus calls him to the cutting edge of his life, as Jesus calls him to discipleship. Do you remember a similar story about Moses before the burning bush? In that story Moses stands there with his sandals off and his knees shaking out of fear as he is being invited into the cutting edge of his life by the Holy One whose name he does not know. He is being called to be the leader of his people.

Where do we find the cutting edges of our lives? Certainly not sitting in front of the television, stretched out for hours, numbed and drugged by the onslaught of images. Certainly not at the mall, buying stuff and more stuff, perhaps to numb the diminishment of meaning in our lives.

So, where does each of us find our cutting edge? I want to answer this question by asking another. What is the Divine will for us? Centuries of sermons have been preached to shed light on this question. Books up to the ceiling and beyond have been written in attempts to answer it. The answer I offer to you today is my personal one: God's will is that we deal creatively and not destructively with our life's menu. The cutting edges of our lives are revealed to us in the items printed on our menus. We need not look elsewhere. Those menus, of course, are always changing. They are different today than they were five, ten, or more years ago, and will be different the same number of years from now.

Sometimes we deal destructively with our menus. For example, we deny what is printed there, or we run away from what is printed there, or we try to change the menu—change that in many cases is not possible. God's Universe and its Earth also have a menu, and it is characterized by change and creativity. The Creative Spirit is present and acting throughout the cosmos and therefore within our lives. It is a Spirit that invites us to participate as co-creators in the cosmic creativity and embrace the Divine promise that our efforts will bear fruit.

Does your life's menu invite you to deal creatively with a challenge within a relationship? Does it invite you to deal creatively with a medical diagnosis that has recently presented itself? Does it invite you to deal creatively with the fact that you are growing older? Does it invite you to deal creatively with our present day catastrophic climate disruption and the diminishment and destruction of Earth's life-systems?

All of these invitations point us to the cutting edges of our lives. These cutting edges are the places where our creativity is called forth, where our faith, hope, and love are required, and where our doubts, anxieties, and fears are to be kept under control. If we listen deeply within while standing on our cutting edges, we can hear the words: Do not be afraid for you have all the gifts you need to deal creatively with your own menu.

# Reflection ∽ Something new

*Do not remember the former things, or consider the things of old. I am about to do a new thing; now it springs forth, do you not perceive it? (Isaiah 43:18-19)*

This message from Isaiah was somewhat strange to the Israelites, as they were a people of memory. It was the memory of Yahweh's mighty past deeds on their behalf, especially leading them out of slavery in Egypt through the desert into a new life in the Promised Land. Isaiah did not throw out the past, but he did call upon the people to look beyond it. They were too dependent on their past, on their tradition, and so they were blind to perceiving the newness that their God was promising and bringing about.

If we look at the story of the Universe we will see that it too is a history defined by change and by newness. 13.7 billion years ago the Universe flared into existence. It was total surprise. It was a newness. 4.5 billion years ago, out of the cosmic dust resulting from the explosion of a star, our planet Earth formed. It was total surprise. It was a newness.

Five hundred and twenty million years ago, responding to evolutionary dynamics, fish emerged within Earth's ocean. It was total surprise. It was a newness. One hundred and thirty million years ago, flowers, in all their colors and fragrances, began to spread across the land. It was total surprise. It was a newness.

Some 200,000 years ago, the first humans, in all their beauty and unpredictability, appeared in East Africa. They were total surprise. They were a newness.

Some 2000 years ago, in Bethlehem of Judea, Jesus of Nazareth was born and later proclaimed God's Reign of justice, peace, and love throughout all of Galilee. He was total surprise. He was a newness.

Whatever your age is today, it was that number of years ago that you floated in the waters of your mother's womb. You were total surprise. You were a newness. There never has been and there never will be another you.

God's Universe values surprise, values newness. What each one of us will create within our lives will be a newness. What our Church will create in this time of its testing will be a newness. What all peoples will do to reverse the withering of Earth's life-systems will be a newness.

We cannot go into the future without our past and our traditions but these cannot lead us there. We need to look beyond the past and not hold on too tightly to it. What leads us into the future are our imaginations, our creativities, our dreams, and our allurements. We are people of the newness that the Divine has promised and the newness that the Divine is bringing about within us: "See, I am doing something new! Do you not perceive it?"

## Reflection ∽ Our deepest desires

*O Lord, how long shall I cry for help and you will not listen...*
*Destruction and violence are before me;*
*strife and contention arise. (Habakkuk 1:2-3)*

Habakkuk is one of the twelve minor prophets of Israel. The dialog between Habakkuk and God follows a pattern that is common to all of the prophets. The first thing that happens is that Habakkuk complains to God, saying that he prays a lot but receives no answers.

One of the duties of a prophet is to be a watchperson. Habakkuk is carrying out this duty. He is watching what is going on in his society. He is reading the signs of the times. As a result he finds himself in circumstances that he experiences to be overwhelming. He cries out to God that there is so much evil and suffering in the land.

Does all this sound familiar? It should! We twenty-first century people also find ourselves in circumstances that are overwhelming. There is economic insecurity, new cancers and diseases, growth in conflicts, and a decrease in the zest for life among many people. We are also beginning to realize that planet Earth itself is suffering much pathology. Like Habakkuk, we too cry out, saying that destruction and violence are everywhere.

After Habakkuk complains God responds to the complaint. God's response takes the form of a vision that is given to the prophet, but we are not told what the vision is. So, the question for us moderns is the following: After all our prayers of petition and all our complaints to God, what is the vision that is given to us? Regardless of our age, each of us has received a vision. For some of us the vision is clear, and for others it is somewhat vague, but the vision is there somewhere deep within. Some questions that can help us to identify our vision are these: For what do we dream? What are our deepest desires? What is alluring us? What is the *more* for which we yearn? For what are we even willing to give our lives?

Is it a fuller life for the children and grandchildren? Better relationships within families? More love and less strife among peoples and nations? A less destructive and a more mutually enhancing relationship between Earth and its human community? Whatever our vision is we need to cherish it. It is a gift that we have received. Whatever our vision is we need to embrace it.

Our vision will lead us into what has been promised. No one wants to drift into the future. We all want to go into it with some sense of direction and purpose. So how do we stir into a flame the vision with which we have been gifted? I offer one simple suggestion. We need to desire deeply that our vision become a reality. We need to begin and end each day of our lives by making that desire our morning and evening prayer. As we pray that our vision be actualized, so shall we act with passion and zest. And slowly but surely, certainly in small ways and perhaps even in some big ways, our vision will become incarnated within our lives and within our Earth.

# Reflection ✑ Cry out in the deserts

*In the wilderness prepare the way of the Lord, make straight in the desert a highway for our God. (Isaiah 40:3)*

The dictionary defines a desert as a wilderness, a dry, barren region and as a parched land without water where there is danger, hardship, and even death for those who lose their way. The desert is where Isaiah says we should prepare.

As we move into this first century of the third millennium we modern people find ourselves living in many wastelands or deserts where daily we experience dangers, hardships, and even deaths.

There are the deserts deep within our own souls such as the desert of hopelessness, the desert of despair, the desert of fear, the desert of discouragement, and the desert of doubt. These deserts are not life-nurturing places. In fact, they can be death places, and to the extent that we live our lives in such wastelands we are indeed more dead than alive.

There are deserts within our Church where sexual abuse of children by priests occurs, where women are denied their proper roles, and where the voices of lay people go unheard. These deserts are not life-nurturing places. In fact, they can be death places, and to the extent that our Church lives in such places it too is indeed more dead than alive.

There are deserts deep within our country, and within other countries as well, where the gap between the rich and the poor grows ever wider, where militarism rules the day and where the legitimate social needs of people are increasingly ignored. These deserts are not life-nurturing places. They can be death places, and to the extent that countries live in such wastelands they are indeed more dead than alive.

There are deserts within Earth. I am not speaking of the geographical deserts of the African Sahara or of the American Southwest. I am speaking of the desert of catastrophic climate disruption, the desert of nuclear wastes, and the desert of ever increasing pollution of air, water, and soil. These deserts are not life-nurturing places. They can be death places, and to the extent that Earth experiences these pathologies Earth is more dead than alive.

A quite different view of deserts is to be found in Scripture. It was in the desert that Israel met Yahweh and that promises were made. That meeting was experienced as shalom or peace. It was also in the desert that Yahweh embraced Israel, made promises, and recovered her love. That recovery was experienced as shalom or peace. The Scripture portrays this loving embrace as causing the desert to blossom.

Each of us, according to our individual talents and strengths, is called to venture into some of the deserts that I have mentioned to prepare the way and bring peace there.

For example, that desert deep within you where you experience only anxiety and fear. Go there and cry out that you are unconditionally loved by God...and experience peace there.

Another example is that desert in our country where the drums of war seem to be always beating and where the Industrial-Military establishment gets money overflowing while the poor and the homeless, the jobless and the uneducated, and the other oppressed of society have their needs increasingly ignored. Go into that desert and make straight a highway for our God by crying out that we are a nation under God and our God is not a God of war but a God of peace and justice…and bring peace and justice into those deserts.

A final example is the desert that is the ever-diminishing vitality of Earth's life-systems. Go into that desert proclaiming that we humans are Earthlings and what we do to Earth we do to ourselves… and bring a blossoming into that desert.

# Reflection *Singing songs of freedom*

> *All the leading priests and the people also were exceedingly unfaithful, following all the abominations of the nations; and they polluted the house of the Lord…. (2 Chronicles 36:14-23)*

As a result of the sinful behavior described in this passage, God's chosen people, who had been led out of slavery in Egypt, found themselves once again taken into slavery. Their enemies had set fire to their Temple and torn down the walls of Jerusalem. The people were now captives in Babylon.

Exile in Babylon meant that the voices they heard, the customs they were forced to obey, the laws they were compelled to observe, were all cruel reminders that their freedom had been forfeited and that they were no longer at home. This experience of captivity was bitter and robbed them of their dignity and joy. By the rivers of Babylon they sat and wept as they remembered their homeland and grieved that they were unable to sing their sacred songs. How they asked, can we sing about what moves most deeply within our souls in this foreign place?

However, after some seventy years in exile, Cyrus, the king of Persia set the people free and rebuilt their Temple in Jerusalem. Once again the people were liberated from slavery and were able to sing their songs. They were born again as a people. Sing a song of freedom sisters! Sing a song of freedom brothers!

Without much effort we can compose a twenty-first century version of this story. In our own time we are adding war upon war, violence upon violence, injustice upon injustice. We are making people of other nations, cultures, and religions our enemies and they are making us their enemies. We are polluting Earth and in the process we are making ourselves toxic. We are worshipping at the altars of the gods of nationalism, individualism, sexism, militarism, consumerism, and a few other gods as well.

The result is that we find ourselves in a twenty-first century Babylon. We have misused our freedom and have chosen death rather than life. Many aspects of our existence have become bitter aspects that rob us of our dignity and our joy. We have spent billions of dollars on the military and yet feel less secure. We have spent millions in our shopping malls and yet find that our lives continue to feel empty. So now we sit by the rivers of our modern Babylon and shed our tears and wonder if it is possible to sing about what moves deeply within our souls.

The answer, of course, is that it is possible. God desires life for us and not death, freedom and not bondage. God is rich in love for us. This love is always being offered, and it carries a justice for Earth and its humans, a promise of greater abundance. All we need do is embrace it.

In this embrace our cries of lamentation will be replaced with songs of joy. We will become sources of love and justice. We will become a blessing for others and for Earth. The promise of more will be realized within us and through us. As a result of this blessing things will never be the same again for Earth and for its humans.

Sing a song of freedom sisters! Sing a song of freedom brothers!

# Reflection ✑ Giving increase

*They went to Capernaum; and when the Sabbath came, he
entered the synagogue and taught. They were astounded at
his teaching, for he taught them as one having authority.
(Mark 1:21-22)*

There is nothing unusual in this story from Mark. Following the custom of his time, Jesus, as an adult male member of the community, took his turn at teaching those gathered in the synagogue. What is unusual is the quality of his teaching. It was so different from that of the scribes who were the official teachers and interpreters of the law. Those gathered in the synagogue recognized this unusual quality. Some marveled at it and perhaps some were disturbed by it.

I want to submit three words for your reflection. They are: author, augment, and authority. Notice that they all begin with the letters "au." This "au" derives from ancient languages and it means "to give increase."

Author…the person who authors a new cookbook makes some new recipes available and thus gives increase to the number of menu possibilities for the home and for the restaurant. Augment…the person who joins a group working to help the homeless augments that group of workers, thus giving increase to its size and effectiveness. Authority…the teacher who teaches in a way that influences, excites, and activates the imaginations of the students is a teacher who gives increase to them.

Many who listened to the teachings of the rabbi Jesus noticed that their lives were enhanced. They were changed by what they heard. They experienced an increase within themselves. True authority is authority that gives an increase, while false authority is authority that gives a decrease.

Parents have authority over their children. They can spoil their children and prevent them from growing into the unique persons they might become, thus giving them a decrease. Or they can encourage the children and give them the space they need to learn, grow, make mistakes, and develop their talents, thus giving them an increase.

Friends and spouses have authority over each other. They can neglect to grow their relationship, thus giving each other a decrease. Or they can strive to nurture and deepen their relationship thus gifting each other with an increase.

The clergy have authority over the laity in the Church. The clergy can put down the laity, treat them as children, and not listen to their advice, thus giving them a decrease. Or the clergy can encourage the laity to take their rightful responsibility and affirm in them the power they have to carry out these responsibilities, thus giving them an increase.

How desperately we modern people need to receive increase in our lives. Some of us are so busy attending to the demands of daily life that we yearn for some small increase as we seek some quiet or meditation time. Many of us are so caught up in our materialistic and consumerist culture that our souls cry out for some increase in meaning and significance.

May we be people of the "au." May we desire each day to be recipients of and givers of increase. May it be a receiving and a giving that will lead us into more abundant life. May it be a receiving and giving that will lead our families, our communities, all of humanity, and Earth itself into the greater abundance that is promised.

# II

# MYSTICS WITH A SMALL "M"

*C⌒⌀*

Generally speaking, when we think of mystics we think of a few select people, such as Teresa of Avila, John of the Cross, or Meister Eckhart. These are Mystics with a large "M." The truth is that each of us is called to be a mystic with a small "m." It is our birthright. It is our destiny.

As charter members of God's Universe, we find ourselves existing within a great emergence, a 13.7 billion year evolutionary story. This Great Story is unfinished and there is much more to come as the Universe continues to unfold into its future. Our personal stories are also unfinished, and there is much more to come as our lives unfold into their futures. So, as we allow this Great Story to wash up on the shores of our consciousness and intertwine with our own stories, we nurture our cosmological sensitivity. As we succeed in doing this, we become mystics…at least with a small "m."

There is a Divine Dynamic that is at work in every aspect of the great emergence. It acts from within the depths of the Universe itself. We humans are growing in our awareness of the entire phenomenal order being infused with and vitalized by this Energy/Spirit. This is indeed good news. No longer need we separate the sacred from the secular and the supernatural from the natural. Our religious imaginations can now, along with Jesuit poet Gerard Manley Hopkins, envision a Universe "charged with the grandeur of God." As we move into this new awareness, we are discovering how blessed we are to be living our lives in such an enchanted place as Earth. As we experience this enchantment we become mystics…at least with a small "m."

Some of the difficulty we have in nurturing a spirituality in which the Divine Dynamic is present and acting within the Universe is because the image of God that resides deep within our religious consciousness is often one of a reality that is "above" or "outside" the Universe. The truth is that God is an "insider" God. There never has been and there never will be a time when the Divine is not embedded in and intimately involved within the Universe, including our own Earth. Divinity resides in and around us. And so we need to consciously embed ourselves in the evolutionary dynamics of the great emergence. As we grow in our ability to find the Divine in all things, we become mystics…at least with a small "m."

**This dynamic of death into life, of breakdown into breakthrough, permeates the Universe and therefore is at work in our own individual lives.**

The evolving Universe can be counted on. It can be trusted. If it has existed 13.7 billion years thus far, why not another 13.7 billion years or more? This great emergence can be trusted because it invites us to search deeper and deeper for truth and beckons us with the promise that such searching is worthwhile and will reveal new and ongoing meaning for our lives. Out of chaos can come new life. This dynamic of death into life, of breakdown into breakthrough, permeates the Universe and therefore is at work in our own individual lives. So, as we learn to trust the deaths of galaxies, stars, and planets, as well as all the dyings in our personal lives, we become mystics…at least with a small "m."

God is intimately involved in the restless adventure that is the Universe, acting by means of a gentle and all-inclusive attraction. It is an attraction into relationship. This cosmic energy of attraction finds its basic expression in the gravitational forces and finds fuller expression in our human capacity to enter into relationships, to enter into love. It should not surprise us that our human sexuality participates in this cosmic allurement. If we can understand and experience our sexuality as that place within us that is hospitable to the cosmic energy of attraction, we become mystics…at least with a small "m."

The mystic Evelyn Underhill described mysticism this way: "The art of union with Reality. The mystic is a person who has attained that union in a greater or lesser degree, or who aims at or believes in such attainment." May it be so for you, and for me.

# Reflection ❧ Burning hearts

*Were not our hearts burning within us*
*while he was talking to us on the road? (Luke 24:32)*

This story in Luke happened during a seven-mile trip that two disciples of Jesus were making from Jerusalem to Emmaus. Our hearts are burning within us today in the twenty-first century on two trips that are much longer than seven miles.

The first trip is the very long journey that the Universe has been making. The second is the adventure of life, of whatever length, that each of us is making. These two are our own "on the road."

Regarding the first, our scientists have determined that the journey of the Universe began some billions of years ago when, out of fertile nothingness, it flared forth into existence. That flaring forth contained the Divine promise of much more to come. And so it happened, over eons of time, that the much more to come was realized as the Universe unfolded galaxies, stars, planets, solar systems, Earth, life, and all of us here on Earth today. We are the first generations of humans ever to know the story of this great unfolding. Our parents probably did not know it, and our grandparents certainly did not know it.

It is a story of billions of years of creative emergence. It is a story that contains all other stories. It is the story of the Universe's unfinished journey, a journey that contains all other unfinished journeys, including our own. There is much more to come as the Universe continues to unfold "on the road" into its future.

The second "on the road" journey is the adventure that is your life and mine. We do not make this trip alone. The promise of much more to come pulsates throughout the Universe and therefore resonates within all of us. So it should not surprise us that we are never satisfied. We carry deep within ourselves an endless aching need for the much more to come. Each of us is an unfinished symphony. Our hearts are restless and whenever we experience this restlessness we are experiencing the Universe's promise of more.

Our individual life adventures are not separate from the Universe's adventure but are a part of it. Our individual and personal "on the road" is part of the Universe's "on the road." We do not journey alone. In fact, it is impossible to journey alone. We journey with everything and everyone that has gone before us and is with us now. Are not our hearts burning? The heart of the mystic constantly burns.

# Reflection ✑ Amazement

*And he rolled up the scroll, gave it back to the attendant and sat down. The eyes of all in the synagogue were fixed on him...and spoke well of him and were amazed at the gracious words that came from his mouth. (Luke 4:20-22)*

Observe baby bears or chimpanzees. They are very playful and curious about everything. They are constantly trying out new things and appear to be amazed at their experiences. It is as if they are saying "awesome" or "cool." Observe human babies. They too are very playful and curious about everything. They are constantly trying out new things and are amazed at their experiences, often to the chagrin and worry of their parents. In their delight, babies often make all kinds of squeaky sounds and, if they could speak, they might say "awesome" or "cool."

When the juvenile bears and chimpanzees mature and move into adulthood, their playfulness and ability to be amazed appears to diminish to a significant extent. They become quite busy finding food, reproducing, and protecting their offspring. As adults they seem to have little time, interest, or involvement with awe, wonder, and amazement.

Not so with us humans. When we move into adulthood, our playfulness and ability to be amazed does not diminish but continues on all the way to the moment of death. As adults, we too become busy working to make money for food, reproducing, and looking after the offspring, but our ability to be amazed, to stand in awe and wonder, remains intact—unless, or course, it is blocked by such forces as despair, loneliness, anger, or depression.

Our ability to be amazed, to be swept off our feet in awe and wonder for a lifetime, is what distinguishes us humans from other animals. It is what opens us up to what is greater than ourselves, to Mystery, to the Divine Dynamic that permeates the Universe.

Remember times in your life when you experienced amazement? Perhaps it was when you were watching moonlight bathing a snow-covered landscape or discovering the immensity of the ocean or feeling the majesty of a mountain. Perhaps you fell in love or were present at the birth of a child. Perhaps you were the recipient of the loyalty of a friend or the wisdom of an elderly person. Perhaps you read or heard some line in a poem or in the Bible, words such as his fellow-Nazarenes heard coming from the mouth of the rabbi Jesus in the story from the Gospel of Luke.

To be amazed, to stand in wonder and awe before all the mysteries of the Universe including our own lives, is the posture of the mystic, even those with a small "m." It is a great grace, an amazing grace, a grace that has brought us this far and will lead us home.

## *Reflection* ᴄᴢ *We are never alone*

*No one will snatch them out of my hand. (John 10:28)*

No one can take us out of God's hands, out of the Divine embrace. We are never alone. This is the promise of Jesus to his followers. Yet we modern people experience much loneliness in our lives. We have even identified such experiences as "existential loneliness" within our human community and "cosmic loneliness" within the unimaginable vastness of the Universe revealed to us by the Hubble telescope.

Let me focus on Earth's air, water, and soil. Our existence is totally dependent upon these elements. If the air is toxic, we who breathe the air become toxic. If the water is toxic, we who drink the water become toxic. If the soil is toxic, we who eat the food grown in that soil become toxic. Yet, generally speaking, we humans do not experience ourselves as being in communion with the air, water, and soil. We tend to experience ourselves as alienated from Earth and its elements, separate from Earth, not an integral part of Earth. Generally speaking, we humans tend to experience ourselves as alone on Earth.

Let me focus on all other people, both those close to us and those at a distance. These others are absolutely necessary for our well-being, in fact, for our very existence. It is only by entering into relationship with others that we discover who we are. By entering into a relationship with its parents, the baby discovers who she or he is. By entering into relationships with other children, the growing child discovers who she or he is. Women and men, by entering into relationships with one another, discover who they are. Peoples of all the nations, by entering into relationship with peoples of other nations, discover their common humanity.

Yet we often experience ourselves as individuals, perhaps even as rugged individuals. We experience ourselves as alienated from others, not really needing them, not really connected to them. Often we value our separateness and devalue our connectedness.

Let me focus now on God, not God at a distance but God within. God is present to us and loving us in and through Earth's air, water, and soil. These elements carry the Divine love for us. God is also present to us and loving us in and through our efforts to enter into and nurture relationships with other people.

We are never alone. When we feel that the Holy One is distant, our feelings do not correspond to reality. In this very moment and in every moment, each of us is in the Divine embrace. We come into existence within that embrace. We live our lives within that embrace. And when we die, we die into that embrace. As we live with this awareness, we become mystics…at least with a small "m."

# *Reflection* ⁓ *Both God and neighbor*

*Mary has chosen the better part which will not be taken away from her. (Luke 10:42)*

How many sermons have been delivered over the centuries on this passage from the Gospel of Luke? How many retreat conferences have been given over the years about Martha and Mary?

Many of us who have heard the sermons or listened to the conferences have gone away thinking that a life spent in a convent or monastery with lots of time for meditation—like Mary—is more valuable than a life spent in the world, raising a family, engaging in business, serving others—like Martha. We have gone away thinking life "in the world" is acceptable, but certainly not as holy as a more contemplative form of life.

This of course, is false. The Second Vatican Council taught us that those of us whose lives are embedded in the world are as authentic disciples of Jesus as those living in convents and monasteries…sometimes more so.

The words placed on the lips of Jesus in this gospel story, therefore, are somewhat unclear. What is this "better part" that Mary has chosen? Is it a life of prayer over a life of action? Is it the things of God over worldly things? There is an un-holy dualism at work in even asking these questions. It is a dualism that separates prayer from action and then ranks prayer as better or higher than action. It is a dualism that separates spiritual things from worldly things and then ranks the spiritual things over worldly affairs.

Such dualistic thinking might have been helpful in the past, but it goes against the grain for us modern women and men of faith who ask: Does loving the world and being concerned about responding to basic human needs make me a second-class citizen within the community of believers?

My personal answer to this is that the story of Martha and Mary immediately follows that of the Good Samaritan in Luke's Gospel. Check your bible. I do not think it is an accident or a coincidence that these two stories are adjacent to each other. The positioning is significant: The two stories are to be read together as one piece, as two peas in the same pod.

The moral of the Good Samaritan story is that we need to get involved and be busy with serving the needs of Earth and its human community. The moral of the Martha and Mary story is that we don't need to be busy at all. All we need do is simply sit in the presence of the Divine who is embedded in the world and in our personal lives, and receive all the love, revelations, and invitations that are available to us there. Both are true. Both postures are required of the mystic…that of serving the neighbor and that of sitting at God's feet and receiving the Divine blessings.

# Reflection ∽ An insider God

> *Are not two sparrows sold for a penny?*
> *Yet not one of them will fall to the ground*
> *apart from your Father. (Matthew 10:29)*

In the religious imaginations of the Hebrew people, and consequently of many Christian people throughout the centuries, God resides at a distance, separate, remote from Earth. God dwells in a heavenly realm somewhere. The Psalms often speak of lifting *up* our eyes, and many present-day prayers speak of sending *down* the Spirit.

As to the knowledge that God has of the sparrow falling to the ground, as found in this parable from Matthew, is it a knowing from the outside or from the inside? Is God a God-at-a-distance or an insider-God-up-close? Does God look down upon the sparrow from above to watch the sparrow fall, or is God present in some way within the sparrow and therefore knows from within about its falling?

Our twenty-first century meditation upon the Universe suggests that there has never been and never will be a time when God is not intimately involved and embedded within the Universe and therefore within our own lives and the life of that fallen sparrow. The Divine is present within the unfolding of the Universe over eons of time. Because of that presence, God knows and feels the joys as well as the sufferings of all creatures from the inside. In the evolving Universe, every being and every activity flows from the Divine Dynamic. The God of our evolutionary Universe is radically committed to cosmic embodiment.

Because our God is an insider God, we can live our lives in the firm faith that God can meet us in any situation and offer new possibilities for the entire human adventure. This offer becomes the basis of our hope, and it is because of this hope that we find the motivation to reach out in love to everyone and everything.

## *Reflection ☙ The Divine initiative*

> *[Moses] rose early in the morning and went up Mount Sinai as the Lord had commanded him…. (Exodus 34:4)*

I call your attention to the fact that it is God who takes the initiative in this story from Exodus. Moses went up the mountain "as the Lord had commanded him." God makes the first move in the encounter.

So often in our spiritual lives we think that we are taking the initiative. In our prayer, for example, we light a candle in our rooms or we go into the church building. We try to quiet ourselves and clear our busy minds. We formulate some words and we speak them. In all of this we perceive ourselves as making the first move. Then we wait for God to reply to our initiative, to make the second move. And we wait some more and some more and some more. Most of the time, however, we do not hear God replying to our prayer and to the dialogue we think we have initiated.

The problem, of course, is that we have reversed the natural order of things. It is the God within who makes the first move, who reveals the Divine presence, who initiates the dialogue with us. It shouldn't surprise us that this is also the order of things throughout the Universe. A star in the night sky first floods us with its light. If you and I are there to receive the light from the star and are open to its initiative, we respond by saying "Awesome." In giving this response, we are making the second move and the encounter between the star and us is now complete.

A flower floods our senses with its color, shape, texture, and fragrance. The flower makes the first move. If you and I are there to receive the flower's self-revelation and are open to its initiative, we respond by saying "How beautiful." In responding, we are making the second move and the encounter between the flower and us is now complete.

The same is true of people. I encounter you because you have first revealed yourself to me. You are radiating light, as everything does. You are making the first move. I perceive the light coming from you and I respond by saying "Hello." In saying this I am responding to your self-revelation. I am making the second move in our encounter.

There is even more going on in our encounter. The light radiating from you reveals to me not only your shape, your size, your height, and other external aspects of you, but it also reveals to me some aspects of your interiority, your personality, your soul.

So let us stand in a posture of openness and anticipation before God and before every person and every thing. In such a posture we allow the others to take the initiative, to flood our souls with their self-revelation. As a result, we are blessed with an amazing grace. It is the gift that enables us to make our response, to make the second move. It is the gift of the mystic.

## Reflection ∕ The voice within

> Surely, this commandment that I am commanding you today
> is not too hard for you, nor is it too far away…it is not up
> in heaven…neither is it beyond the sea…No, the word is
> very near to you; it is in your mouth and in your heart….
> (Deuteronomy 30:10-14)

An important word in this passage from Deuteronomy is "in." We are accustomed to imagining God as being on the outside, up above somewhere, occasionally coming down and intervening in what is happening here on Earth and within our lives and then leaving again.

Yet according to Deuteronomy, the Divine voice is not without. It is very near. In fact, it is within each of our hearts and therefore within the whole Universe because the Universe has unfolded us. And, of course, where God's voice is there God is.

We need to get in touch with our "withins." The Divine voice speaks there. God's wisdom is to be found there. We can know everything that is required for living justly and lovingly. It is within every one of us to have such deep knowledge and wisdom.

Find your within. It is that place deep in you that makes you the unique person and the one-time and unrepeatable event in the Universe that you are. It is that place deep in you where you are wise. It is that place deep inside of you where the Holy One speaks.

Only in the last few decades we have learned that God's Universe came into existence some billions of years ago and has been unfolding ever since, unfolding into greater variety of different creatures, into greater depths of consciousness within creatures, and into greater inter-connections among creatures. Only in the last few decades we have learned that we humans carry that creativity within ourselves. This is a new wisdom that resides in our withins.

It has only been in the past two thousand years or so that we members of the Christian community have nurtured within ourselves the consciousness of Jesus. He took the wisdom that he inherited from his tradition—from Abraham and Sarah, from Moses and Miriam, and from all the prophets. Jesus took this endowment and raised it to a more inclusive and cosmic level. His consciousness, his wisdom, is available to each of us in our withins and therefore is available to all of humankind in its within.

As I write to you out of my depths and as you receive my words in your depths our withins are nourishing each other. When our withins touch in this way we are experiencing that kind of communion that mystics experience.

The Ten Commandments are something external, but by reflecting on our own human experience each one of us knows deep within that we should not steal, lie, commit adultery, or treat our parents badly.

By reflecting on our own human experience, each one of us knows deep within that we need to understand and respect all those people, cultures, and religions that are different from us. Each one of us knows deep within that we need to stand in reverence and awe before the withins of all creatures.

Such deep-within knowledge makes each of us a mystic…at least with a small "m."

# III

# THE IMMENSITIES

T hroughout my adult years, I have observed other men spending time with their families out in the backyard, cooking burgers on the grill or just relaxing in the shade of a tree. I have often found myself being envious of them, as they seemed to be living neither in the past nor in the future but totally absorbed in the present moment with all the blessings it has to offer them. They seem to be in what I would call a "micro-phase" place and are happy to be there.

Not so with me. When I am sitting in the shade under a tree, the present moment often evades me as I ponder and wrestle with the large and pressing issues of the day. It is the ecological and cosmological ones that tend to capture my attention these years. It seems that my preferred places in which to reside are in "macro-phase" places, such as contemplating the meaning of life or the history of the Universe, and most of the time I am content to be there. Perhaps it is more correct to say that I don't seek out such places but that they seek me out.

Another way to describe my propensity for macro-phase places is to say that I have always been allured by "the immensities." As an early adolescent, I was enthralled by stars of the night sky, mountains, oceans, and moonlight on water. These experiences, and others like them, revealed to me that I was part of and informed by something much larger than myself. They revealed that the inner and the outer worlds were in some mysterious way one and that the meaning of my life was somehow embedded in these immensities. I knew all of these truths in some deep intuitive way, but at such a young age I had very few words to give voice to my experiences.

As an adult, however, the immensities—both the outward and the inward ones—have become my spiritual guides. They invited me to move out of a narrow consciousness into a more comprehensive one. By contemplating the Universe, my small self discovered that it resided within a Great Self. The mystery of my own existence was revealed as a facet of Ultimate Mystery. These experiences were exciting and sometimes terrifying. They always made a difference in how I view things, and they continue to do so.

**The contemplation of the immensities invite us into wonder, and then into mystery.**

I often wonder if the contemplation of the immensities can do this for all human beings. They invite us into wonder, and then into mystery. It seems to me that the origin and unfolding of religion itself is to be found in such experiences of wonderfulness and mysteriousness. These encounters with Ultimate Mystery become a blessing, a gift, and as a result of this giftedness we are changed. Life can never be the same for us.

Some say that this emphasis on the universal can blind us to the particular. They say that focusing on the whole picture can prevent us from a full engagement with its parts. I suspect people fear that the immensities might blind us to the enormous problems and challenges presented to us in this twenty-first century. Such blindness is indeed a possibility. On the other hand, an awareness of the universal can prevent us from getting fixated on what is fragmentary. Among the fragments are militarism, nationalism, sexism, fundamentalism, individualism, elitism, and consumerism. A life and culture focused on such fragments can become a life and a culture caught-up in what is ultimately ephemeral.

Contemplation of the immensities places us within our proper context as humans. Humility replaces arrogance. We are led to experience ourselves as cosmological and planetary people. We are freed from the impulse to dominate, utilize, and possess. We are freed for living not on the surface but deeper down, in that place where our true potential as individuals and as a species waits to be activated.

Others say that standing amidst the immensities might make us feel good but changes little or nothing. My experience is that such awareness changes everything. It gives us a way out of the pathos of our times. It evokes hope. It gives us new answers to the ancient question: What does it mean to be human? We are that life species whose genetic and cultural endowment carries billions of years of creativity. Like the evolving Universe itself, we are an unfulfilled potential and carry depths of possibilities. We are, according to cultural historian Thomas Berry, "That species in whom the universe reflects on and celebrates itself and its numinous origins in a special mode of conscious self-awareness."

In exploring the relationships between humans, Earth, and the Creative Power of the Universe, we are led into a wisdom that illuminates our efforts to educate our children, to do economics in a new way, and to bring about greater justice for Earth and its humans. Upon embracing these truths we find ourselves participating in a great transformation of consciousness. It is the beginning of an evolutionary leap forward for humankind.

Meditation on the immensities is meditation on those numinous places where the Divine and the human engage each other. The story of the Universe is the story of God's presence and action within the vastness of the macro-phase and consequently within the intimacy of the micro-phase. Those guys at their grills in their backyards with their families are part of a cosmological movement of life, whether they realize it or not.

And if they do realize it, then the immensities will allure them into an ecological concern for Earth as a whole and for each local manifestation of that whole. They will be invited into an ethic that is more universal, one that includes but looks beyond the social, economic, political, and religious realms. The immensities will awaken their imagination and sharpen their sense of beauty. They will find themselves in cosmic time, within which primordial hydrogen becomes all the other chemical elements and an early molten Earth becomes this present moment, including their lovely and holy backyard picnics.

## *Reflection ⁊ Abundance*

> *You prepare a table before me…you anoint my head with oil; my cup overflows. (Psalm 23:5)*

"You prepare a table before me." In the Middle East to this very day there are sheiks, Arab chiefs, who live in large tents in the desert and prepare lavish banquets for their guests. In your imagination, picture such a tent containing a large rug upon which has been spread many lovely things to eat and drink. See all of the food items in their variety. There is such abundance, an abundance that you would not expect to find in the desert.

"You anoint my head with oil." Semitic men in ancient times generally wore a full beard and cultivated it with great care. Aaron, the brother of Moses, for example, had such a beard when he was anointed high priest using olive oil. In your imagination see the scene as it is described: "…precious oil upon the head, running down upon the beard, upon the beard of Aaron, running down on the collar of his robes" (Psalm 133:2).

"My cup overflows." You might picture a cup of coffee or tea overflowing. My favorite image comes from an ice cream parlor that I frequented as a high school and college student. The place was famous for its ice cream sundaes and the cups in which they were served. In your imagination see a silver plated cup for holding the ice cream sitting on top of a long silver plated stem leading down to a silver plated dish. See the cup holding a generous amount of ice cream covered with hot fudge that is overlaid with marshmallow and nuts. See the mixture slowly dripping down from the cup onto the plate below.

Consider that there are a hundred billion galaxies in the Universe, with each galaxy containing on the average a hundred million stars. It has been determined by our scientists that each second our Sun burns up and transforms approximately four million tons of itself into light and heat energy and a small amount of that energy reaches Earth, bathes us, and makes life possible. And think about the number of times throughout eons of time that our Earth has turned toward its Sun, causing morning, and has turned away from its sun, causing night.

It has been estimated that there are approximately a quadrillion molecules of air entering into your lungs at this moment bringing about the continuance of your life. A quadrillion! That's the number one followed by twenty-four zeros.

Consider the abundance of love parents and grandparents have poured out and are pouring out into the lives of their children and grandchildren.

Try to count the number of times in your life that you have prayed, meditated, and worshiped. Ponder how God loved you when you were only a possibility in the Universe and when you first foamed into existence within your mother's womb. At every moment of your life since then you have been in the Divine embrace.

## *Reflection* ❧ *The primary revelation*

> *In the time of King Herod, after Jesus was born in Bethlehem of Judea, wise men from the East came to Jerusalem, asking "Where is the child who has been born king of the Jews?" (Matthew 2:1-2)*

The magi were professionals when it came to relating to the stars. They related to them not as objects to be studied but as subjects that had some truth to reveal. The "Three Kings" were experienced when it came to allowing their own wisdom to interact with the wisdom of the stars. They searched for truth in the wonders of the Universe. They were not afraid to search, because their expectation was that the search would result in enlightenment regarding the meaning of life here on Earth.

The star that led them across the desert to Jerusalem spoke to them of the birth of a new King. They were overjoyed at, not threatened by, this revelation. After finding the infant King and paying him homage, they returned to the East from where they had come. For them, the journey was worth it. They returned home changed and enriched.

We believers in this first century of the third millennium need to embrace the lesson of the magi. There is a strand in the fabric of our Christian tradition that is suspicious of the stars, trees, plants, even other animals. The natural world is not a side trip off the main road to God or, even worse, an obstacle on the road to God. It is the way to God.

The marvelous truth is that the only knowledge we have of the

Creator is through our experience of the Creation. Each and every creature we humans encounter has its own inner truth. The entire Universe—from the farthest galaxy to the smallest atomic particle, from the rivers and the prairies to the entire animal kingdom including us humans—reveals something of the Divine Dynamic and offers some enlightenment about the meaning of our lives.

Like the magi, we twenty-first century believers need to be attentive to the powers and mysteries of the Universe. In so doing we will be blessed. Our individual lives will be enriched and as a result the entire Earth community will be blessed.

This blessing will be a gift for us, not of gold, frankincense, or myrrh, but an experience of God's primary revelation.

# *Reflection* ☙ *Cathedral building*

> *Let us go on to the neighboring towns, so that I may proclaim the message there also; for that is what I came out to do.*
> *(Mark 1:38)*

There is a story that has its origins in medieval Europe. It is the story of three masons who were working on a cathedral. The first was asked what he was doing and he replied that he was cutting stones. The second, when asked the same question, replied that he was supporting his family. The third, when asked, said that he was giving glory to God.

Like the third man, Jesus realized that he had a great work. He was building something. This was why he was anxious to preach and teach in all the villages. This was his life's purpose. He was pouring out his energies into announcing and inaugurating what he called the Kingdom or Reign of God. His vision for this world was that it would experience an increasing amount of justice, peace, and love because of how his followers would live their lives. This was his cathedral, his great work.

What is our great work? What is the cathedral that we are build-ing at the beginning of this twenty-first century? I wish to focus on two cathedrals that we are being called to build.

The first has to do with the drums of war that each day beat ever so loudly in our ears and in our souls. The willingness of nations to incur massive military expenditures seems to stand in sharp con-trast to their unwillingness to promote the sustainable development of the world, a world of growing inequalities, where the majority of human beings lack what they need to live with basic dignity. In 1965, Pope Paul VI spoke at the United Nations and proclaimed for all of humanity to hear: "No more war, war never again." This is a cathedral we need to be building. This is our great work.

The second cathedral actually contains the first, because it is more comprehensive and overarching. It has to do with our ever-increasing disruption of the community of life here on Earth. We are releasing toxins into the atmosphere. Our children are breathing in those toxins, with the result that childhood asthma and other respira-tory diseases have already reached an all-time high. We are dumping toxins into the ocean waters. That same toxic water makes its way into mothers' wombs, and the babies in those wombs are being born sick. We are pouring poisons into the soil, poisons that make their way into the food grown in that soil. Toxological studies of our food supply are few and far between, with the result that an increasing number of children are experiencing the weakening of their immune systems. Cancer, once an adult disease, is now prevalent among our children.

In 1990, Pope John Paul II proclaimed for all to hear: "There is an order in the universe that must be respected, and the human person has a grave responsibility to preserve this order for the well-being of fu-ture generations." The preservation of this order, this mutually enhanc-ing relationship between Earth and its humans, is our great work.

The third man was asked: "What are you doing?" He replied: "I am giving glory to God." Sisters and brothers, what is the cathedral that we are building?

# Reflection ∽ Cosmic mothering

*The good shepherd lays down his life for the sheep. (John 10:11)*

Sheep do not take care of themselves very well. Unlike other livestock, sheep require endless attention and care. That is why they need a good shepherd. A good shepherd is gentle, brave, and selfless in his or her devotion to the flock with the result that the sheep thrive.

For a good shepherd there is no greater reward, no deeper satisfaction, than that of seeing the sheep well fed, contented, and safe. This is the vocation of a shepherd, and a good one, as Jesus suggested, gives all he or she has to it.

But wait! Have I been speaking about shepherds or about mothers?

Human children do not take very good care of themselves. Unlike the young of most other mammals, human children require endless attention and care for many years. A good mother is gentle, brave, and selfless in her devotion to her children. She is willing to lay down her life for them. For a good mother there is no greater reward, no deeper satisfaction, than seeing her children well fed, contented, and safe. This is her vocation, and she gives all she has to it.

But wait! Have I been speaking about human mothers or about our Earth Mother?

Our Earth Mother is on the job twenty-four hours a day attending to the needs of her human children. She will go to any end to supply these needs. From early dawn and throughout the night she provides us with fresh air to fill our lungs with its oxygen for the functioning of our various organs. She supplies fresh water that quenches our thirst and supplies the essential elements we require for most of the chemical reactions that take place in our bodies.

Our Earth Mother supplies the calcium, phosphorus, zinc, magnesium, and other minerals that we need for our bones and well-being. She gifts us with an endless variety of shapes, colors, odors, sounds, and textures that delight our senses and stimulates our imaginations. She nurtures our innate sense of the Divine.

May we give thanks for our human mothers and our Earth Mother. May we remember, celebrate, and give thanks for all the shepherding we have received from them in our lives.

## *Reflection* ⟋ *Vineyards*

*My beloved had a vineyard on a very fertile hill.*
*He dug it up and cleared it of stones.*
*And planted it with choice vines.... (Isaiah 5:1-7)*

The vineyard in this poem from the prophet Isaiah refers to the House of Israel, upon which Israel's "friend," Yahweh, had lavished so much care, commitment, and love.

A number of years ago I lived in California and made several driving trips up into the wine country. It was awesome! Imagine the rolling hills covered with miles of parallel rows of vines. They look like an army marching in formation. See the vines, hundreds of thousands of them, growing vertically on a stake or trellis up onto a wire above. It is a wonderful sight. So much care and commitment goes into a vineyard, so much pouring out of time, energy, and love goes into the nurturing of a vineyard.

There are, of course, other vineyards. One is located deep within each of us. It is our inner-self. This vineyard requires our loving commitment, especially in our consumer culture that constantly pushes us to live superficially and materially rather than deeply and spiritually.

Another vineyard is our family-and-friends-self. It is the first circle out from our inner-self. This vineyard also requires our loving commitment, especially at the beginning of this twenty-first century when many of our close relationships are under stress from a culture of individualism, competitiveness, and workaholism.

Another vineyard, the next circle out, is our church-self. This vineyard also requires our loving commitment, especially at this time when pronouncements coming down from on high seem to ignore the lived experience of the faithful.

Another vineyard, the next circle out, is our national-self. This vineyard especially requires our loving commitment at this time when our country is suffering from a loss of identity and is questioning its role in the community of nations.

Another vineyard, the next circle out, is our Earth-self. This vineyard requires our loving commitment, especially at this time of Earth's withering, a withering that involves global warming, the disrupting and diminishing of the web of life, and many other pathological conditions.

Finally, the outermost circle is the vineyard that is our Universe-self. It contains all our other selves. It is a sacred place within us that houses all the immensities, a place where we can contribute to a cosmic nurturing and caring.

All of these vineyards, all of these selves, are sacred places where we are working out our "Yes" to life and our "Yes" to God. They are vineyards where good grapes can be produced and where justice, peace, and love can grow in abundance.

# Reflection ✐ Moved with pity

*As he went ashore, he saw a vast crowd; and he had*
*compassion for them, because they were like sheep without a*
*shepherd.... (Mark 6:34)*

In this story from Mark, people were coming to Jesus in great numbers, seeking to be cured and searching for something more in their lives. They were making endless demands on him and his disciples. So he and the disciples went off in a boat by themselves to a deserted place, a place where they thought they could rest for a while. The crowds, however, had figured out their plan and were waiting for them when they arrived.

There are many people seeking and searching in our modern world today. They could be parents of a seriously sick child, elderly people who are feeling a diminishment within their bodies, widows and widowers who live alone, street persons, women and men without jobs, or young people questioning society's values. The list, of course, goes on and on.

I want to move our focus onto the level of being concerned about what Earth is seeking from its human community.

We citizens of the U.S.A. like to sing the patriotic song "God Bless America" with its words, "From the mountains, to the prairies, to the ocean, white with foam." The reality is that the mountains are being denuded of their trees with the result that their soils are eroding away. The prairies, through our extensive use of industrial chemicals, are being forced to produce crops beyond their natural capacity to do so, with the result that their soils are depleted of minerals and other nutrients. The ocean is no longer white with foam but is increasingly yellow and brown, with foam laced with toxins of all descriptions, including crude oil that we spill from tankers and wells.

The reality is that the biodiversity of Earth and the vitality of its life systems are under great stress. The atmosphere is warming. Salt water is encroaching on the land as the ocean is rising. Deserts are expanding. Mother's milk among arctic Eskimos and among Antarctic penguins contains high and unacceptable levels of lead, mercury, DDT, and PCB's. Among human children, cancers, respiratory diseases, and immune system breakdowns are increasing at an alarming rate. Earth, including its human community, cries out for some attention and care.

It is no accident that we are living at this time in Universe history. As twenty-first century people, following in the way of Jesus, Earth is crying out for our care. We may think we are too tired or at least deserve to get away for a while. Remember, however, that when Jesus saw the crowds "his heart was moved with pity for them." So he canceled his rest day and went to work. So too must our hearts go out to Earth, which needs our help and needs it now. Earth is the neighbor that Jesus invites to love as we love ourselves.

# IV

## SOUL SIZE

*C∽*

Approximately a million years ago, long before what we ego-centric humans have called "ancient history," our ancestors learned how to control fire. With this breakthrough a whole new set of possibilities were activated. Language and culture emerged. Things would never be the same again for us.

A mere two thousand years ago, Jesus of Nazareth took the teachings he had received from his Jewish tradition and moved them to a new level of understanding. This newness, this all-inclusive way of loving, now became available to the whole human community as many women and men sensed life in greater abundance was to be found in the practice of this kind of loving.

In 1948, the British astronomer Fred Hoyle said: "Once a photograph of the Earth, taken from the outside, is available...a new idea as powerful as any in history will be let loose." And so it happened. In the late sixties we left our planet, got outside, looked back, and saw Earth as it really is. We were the first humans ever to view Earth from space. A new level of consciousness emerged within our planet. Things would never be the same again for Earth and its human community.

The image is shattering. Earth is piercingly beautiful, a blue and white pearl suspended in the darkness of space. So delicate. So fragile in its appearance. Unlike anything else we are aware of in the Universe. Not an object but a living subject. A physical reality to be sure, but also a spiritual one. It carries not only the stuff of our bodies but also the dimensions of our minds and spirits. It carries everything that means anything to us. It is a sacred place.

This is the new idea that has been set loose. Mystics and indigenous peoples have always known it. For us moderns it is a revelation. Our scientific endeavor—the work of cosmologists, astronomers, physicists, geologists, biologists, anthropologists, and others—has been its messenger. The message has come at an opportune time, a time when we are trashing our planet on a scale beyond imagining and certainly beyond our capacity to fully measure. Earth is saying to us: "See how destructive you are being, both to me and to yourselves. It is an illusion for you to think that you are separate from me. We constitute a whole. Everything and everyone is interconnected. I am not merely a backdrop for your human adventure. I am the womb within which that adventure unfolds."

**Not only your hand but also your heart and the meaning of your life are intimately woven within the fabric of the Universe.**

Look at your hand. How old is it? It is as old as the Universe. It took that long to form your hand. Everything that has happened in the Universe from its beginning has influenced the shaping of your hand. The protons in your hand were made in the primordial fireball. The atoms there once floated in a galactic cloud that resulted from the supernova explosion of a star. The whole sequence on Earth of the shaping of life in the ocean, the development of life on land, and the millions of years of biological trial and error, have all contributed to the formation of your hand. To know the story of your hand is to be filled with wonder and humility at how the Universe has formed you. It is to know that not only your hand but also your heart and the meaning of your life are intimately woven within the fabric of the Universe, within the Whole.

The Whole is a problem for us modern humans. Our mechanistic view of reality causes us to think mainly in terms of parts. We have difficulty in thinking holistically even about our personal health not to mention the planetary health. Our minds and imaginations are focused too narrowly, focused to the point that we think a hand is only a hand.

Yet the Whole is calling out to us. Our problems are planetary problems. We have named several oceans, but in reality there is only one ocean. To pollute a part of it is to pollute all of it. There are no borders. Acid rain falls on countries that do not cause it. Our chemical assault on Earth's gene pool will affect future generations of all life forms. The weakening of Earth's immune system and the human immune system are related pathologies.

Nor are we without the necessary tools for changing things. General Systems Theory assists us to think of wholes rather than parts. The Gaia Hypothesis allows us to view Earth as a living whole. The New Cosmology instructs us that our individual-self is unfolding within our Earth-self which is unfolding within our Universe-self. We now have our icon of Earth as seen from space.

Cultural historian Thomas Berry, using an Exodus motif, spoke of the Whole: "The human community and the natural world will go into the future as a single sacred community or we will both experience severe difficulties in the desert."

The Creative Energy of the Universe moves within us and is awakening us. Earth has placed much responsibility into our hands. The future is pressing into the present moment. What will we humans choose? Our choices are definitely soul size. What that means is that our ability to solve our problems will be limited by the size of our collective soul.

# Reflection ✑ A great turning

*In those days John the Baptist appeared in the wilderness of Judea proclaiming "Repent, for the kingdom of heaven has come near"…. (Matthew 3:1-2)*

At the time of the Baptist, repentance showed itself in external signs such as fasting, public lamentations, loud cries, cutting oneself, wearing sackcloth and ashes, and the public confession of sins. These external signs indicated an internal disposition or change of heart, a rejection of one's past life, and a radical turning about. This is the deepest meaning of the word "repent." It means not just a minor change in direction but a 180-degree turn from one's previous path.

The Baptist proclaimed that such a serious turning was required as preparation for the dawning of a new age. The question before us today at the beginning of the twenty-first century is: What kind of serious turning is required of humanity as we engage with the new age that is dawning within our time?

I want to share with you my answer to this question. I was ten years old in 1945 when the U.S.A. dropped the atomic bomb on the Japanese city of Hiroshima, killing in an instant some 140,000 innocent civilians. Three days later, we dropped another bomb on the city of Nagasaki, killing some 70,000 non-combatants. Those two events had a deep effect upon my young psyche. I didn't have any words for it at that time, but deep inside I knew that biocide was a possibility…not homicide or suicide or genocide but biocide…the killing of vast sections of the community of life here on Earth.

No previous humans have ever possessed such power, a power once accorded only to the gods. In 1945 the United States was the only nation with a nuclear weapon. Today there are many. The possibility of nuclear biocide has increased enormously in modern times, but it does not seem to loom large in our collective consciousness. Perhaps it is something just too horrible for humans to think about. Perhaps we are paralyzed by the thought.

Even apart from this nuclear danger, however, biocide is well underway. Earth's forests are shrinking, water-tables are falling, soils are eroding, fisheries are collapsing, rivers are running dry, glaciers and ice caps are melting, coral reefs are dying, plant and animal species are going into extinction, and human children are increasingly dying of malnutrition, cancer, and immune system breakdowns. Earth and its life-community are under increasing stress. Life forms are approaching a precipice with increasing speed. No previous generations have ever had to deal with this danger. They couldn't even have imagined the present day pathological situation of our planet.

This is a time that calls out to us to repent, to make a radical turn away from the precipice we are beyond any doubt headed for. Never before has such a collective change of heart been required of humanity.

This need for repentance is a primary sign of our times, no less than it was in the time of John the Baptist. It is a sign that should move all of Earth's people into action. It is a sign that calls upon us to be not just economic, political, and religious people but also planetary people. On the level of soul we are called to be such people.

# *Reflection* ⌖ *Consciousness evolving*

*The spirit of the Lord God is upon me, because the Lord
has anointed me; he has sent me to bring good news to the
oppressed, to bind up the brokenhearted, to proclaim liberty to
the captives.... (Isaiah 61:1)*

Jesus of Nazareth appeared some five hundred years after Isaiah. He
taught that the "brokenhearted" and the "captives" are not only the
Jews but also the Gentiles. According to Jesus, each and every person
is our neighbor, who is to be loved by us as we love ourselves. Even
the enemy and the worshipper of false gods is the neighbor to be
loved. Even the person who curses us and says all kinds of bad things
about us is the neighbor to be loved. What an advance in consciousness this was on the part of Jesus.

Something similar happened to each of us when we were in-
fants. Sometime during our second or third month we went from
experiencing the world as being a two-dimensional world to experiencing it as having a third dimension, that of depth. What a growth in
consciousness this was on our part. We went from seeing everything
as flat to seeing the depths of things.

Several months later in our infancy we became aware that our
world wasn't just our mothers and us, but also contained our fathers,
brothers, sisters, and others. What a growth in consciousness this
was. We moved from living in a two-person universe into a multiple-
person one.

A similar unfolding in consciousness occurred when we moved
into adolescence, and for many of us these quantum leaps in consciousness have occurred throughout our lives and hopefully will
continue to do so.

At the beginning of this century, another expansion of our consciousness is under way. We are just beginning to work at cleaning up polluted rivers and lakes, replanting forests, and trying to reduce the emission of planet warming gases into the atmosphere. All of these— the rivers, lakes, forests, and atmosphere—are "neighbors" that need to be loved. What a growth in consciousness this requires of all of us. We are moving from a human-centered consciousness into a planetary one.

## Reflection ✑ Prophets of Earth

> *And when he spoke to me, the spirit entered into me and set me on my feet.... (Ezekiel 2:2)*

It was in the sixth century before Jesus while the Israelites were in exile as slaves in Babylon that the priest Ezekiel was reading the "signs of the times." The signs of the times are those deep movements rising from within peoples and nations, movements that come from the depths of the human soul.

Because the Spirit was within him, Ezekiel was able to perceive the Spirit that was moving within his own people. They were experiencing a helplessness and hopelessness. They were feeling that God had abandoned them. The result of all of this was that they were beginning to drift away from their God.

Ezekiel knew that he was being called to serve his people in their dire situation. From deep within, he knew that he must speak the truth and not some sweet-sounding message that would temporally numb his people to their pain. He also knew that there was no guarantee that they would listen to his message. However, in the face of all possible opposition, Ezekiel knew that the Divine was moving within him and would supply him with the strength he needed to carry out his mission.

During the twentieth century, large numbers of Earth's people were not independent but lived their lives trapped in colonial structures. These people were also reading the signs of their times. They perceived a restlessness moving within themselves that came from the depths of their souls. It was their desire to be free of the colonial bonds, to have greater freedom, to have their own place in the Sun. And so it happened that during that same century political independence was achieved by most of them.

Today, in our twenty-first century, the peoples of the world, the citizens of Earth, are beginning to read a new sign of the times. This new sign can be described as a helplessness and hopelessness arising from their growing awareness of the withering of Planet Earth and its life-systems. Yes, Earth is withering! Ever-increasing numbers of us—those who are not in denial and choose not to bury their heads in the sand—are becoming aware of the pathological planetary condition and desire to do something about it.

Like Ezekiel, from deep within we are beginning to realize that we are being called, that we are being sent to be prophets of Earth in its time of dire need. From deep within we know that the truth of the Earth's cry for help must be proclaimed aloud. It is Earth's truth. As Earthlings, it is our truth. And we must avoid the temptation to speak a sweet-sounding message so that people can feel better. We must confront the withering of our Earth. Only this truth will set us free.

In doing this we, like Ezekiel, will face opposition. Some will say that we are exaggerating or that we are pessimists and alarmists. But speak we must, knowing that the Spirit will "set us on our feet" and provide us with the energy to carry out this prophetic mission to which we have been called.

# Reflection ⟳ The depths of things

> *Blessed are those who trust in the Lord, whose trust is the Lord. They shall be like a tree planted by water, sending out its roots by the stream.... (Jeremiah 17:7-8)*

Jeremiah had this inspiring image of a tree planted near the waters of a stream with its roots pushing deep down into the moist soil. Such a tree does not fear the heat, and its leaves remain green. Such a tree is not damaged by the drought and continues to bear much fruit.

It has been determined by scientists that some two million years ago our human ancestors learned to control fire. Let us imagine the scene out on the plains of East Africa. A storm is approaching and a bolt of lightning strikes a tree causing it to burst into flames. Let us imagine that some chimpanzees and early humans witnessed this event. The chimpanzees turn and run. Some of our human ancestors turn and run, but others do not.

Those humans who do not run are curious. They draw closer to the flame and perhaps even burn themselves. They notice that the "fire," as they call it in whatever language they had, gives off heat. One of them realizes that the "fire" might be used to cook their food, perhaps after tasting a burnt piece of meat from an animal that had been caught in the "fire." Others notice that the "fire" gives off light and could provide some illumination in the darkness of their caves at night. Perhaps an artist or two among them gazes deeply into the "fire" and notices that memories and desires are evoked in them by the flames.

Humans have 98.6% the same genes as do the chimpanzees. It is that slightly more than 1% that makes the difference between running from the flames and not running, that makes it possible for us humans to be curious, to be fascinated, to notice, to imagine, to look deeply.

We humans are that species that is able to comprehend the depths of things. We are like the tree planted in the moist soil. We can extend our roots deeply to make contact with the challenges and meanings that are embedded there and the Mystery that is embedded there.

I remember watching a documentary film about the historic march to Montgomery that occurred back in the early sixties in Alabama. This march happened because of a previous march, during which hundreds of African Americans were beaten with night sticks and gassed by the police. All of this was televised nationally. The images of such brutality, such overt racism, raw violence, and stark hatred evoked an outpouring of responses. Thousands of people of all races, religions, and political orientations from all parts of our country joined a second march to Montgomery. Priests, rabbis, ministers, nuns, professors, laborers, office workers, housewives, boy scouts and students marched.

Like the tree planted near the waters, these "outsiders," as they were called, were able to extend their roots deeply into the souls of black Americans in Alabama. As a result of that march, the lives of all our citizens, black and white, were changed. Things would never be the same in our country again.

What does it mean to be human? It means to capture the depths of things.

# Reflection ∽ Newness out of chaos

*There will be signs in the sun, the moon, and the stars, and on the earth distress among nations confused by the roaring of the sea and the waves. (Luke 21:25)*

"There will be signs in the sun, the moon, and the stars"…these are cosmic signs.

There are two cosmic signs of which we are increasingly aware. They both concern the relationship between our Sun and its Earth.

First, due to the diminishment of Earth's ozone layer, the Sun's harmful ultraviolet radiation is getting through to the planet's surface in greater amounts. This results in present-day planet-wide problems for humans and other life forms, and it guarantees future chaos within Earth's community of life. Second, due to the build-up of greenhouse gases caused to a significant extent by the burning of fossil fuels, Earth's climate is becoming warmer and the polar icecaps and glaciers are melting. This present day catastrophic climate disruption guarantees future disasters and future chaos.

"And on earth distress among nations"…these are national signs.

In the majority of nations today, the economic, legal, medical, educational, and religious structures are under increasing stress and in some cases are in the process of collapsing. In our own country the economy is such that the gap between the rich and the poor is growing ever wider. Our legal system is unbalanced, as the rich are regularly declared innocent while the poor are regularly incarcerated. Our health care structures make the latest medical advances available only to those who can pay extra, while many wait in lines at hospital emergency rooms for whatever treatment they can get.

Our educational institutions have become less places of learning and more places of violence. Some of our religious institutions are drifting into a fundamentalism while others are becoming a scandal to their own members. All of these structural pathologies speak of increasing chaos in our nation.

"Confused by the roaring of the sea and the waves"…these are ecological signs.

Everywhere on Earth waters are polluted, air is increasingly dangerous to breathe, and soils are eroded and chemically contaminated. Biotic communities are disrupted, life-species are going into extinction, and immune systems are not working properly. The entire web of life is under stress. All of this present chaos points to increasing future chaos for Earth and its humans.

Scientists who study the Universe as a whole tell us about a process that has been going on throughout the entire 13.7 billion years of its existence. It is a process where things break down and enter into chaos. The chaos is then followed by a breakthrough, a creative emergence of something new. Not only do we need to see the cosmic, national, and ecological breakdowns that are happening at the present time, we also need to expect that over time something new will creatively emerge from out of them.

So, we need not be fearful in the midst of such soul size challenges. We need not slip into paralysis and say that the challenges are too much and there is nothing we can do about them. We need to remind ourselves that the Creative Spirit is present and at work within the Universe and therefore within each of us. As women and men of faith, we need to be convinced that something new will emerge out of the breakdowns and chaos. Perhaps we presently cannot see clearly what the newness will be, but it will happen.

# Reflection ⌒ Living as a creative word

*And see, I am sending upon you what my Father promised; so stay here in the city until you have been clothed with power from on high. (Luke 24:49)*

Billions of years ago that "power from on high" that Jesus talked about, that Creative Word, was spoken within the void, and energy flared forth out of that emptiness. The energy was followed by atoms, by galaxies, and by stars as numerous as the sands on the seashore. Over deep time it was followed by our solar system with its beautiful planet Earth, and finally by Earth's human community.

Some 2000 years ago that Creative Word was spoken again and became enfleshed in Jesus of Nazareth. His short life was full of life. In obedience to what he was called to do and what he was called to be, he traveled around to the towns and villages of his own country, preaching in the synagogues, at lakesides, and on mountaintops. He also did a lot of healing. He embraced the conflicts, misunderstandings, and sufferings that came his way, all the way to his death on a cross.

Jesus emerged from his death transformed. He is now where he has always been, namely, in the embrace of the Divine. He is there, we Christians believe, in some new or resurrected way.

Each of us is that Creative Word, spoken and enfleshed. Each of us is a Word spoken for a lifetime that does not return to God empty. The reason we do not return empty is that we are co-creators. Yes, co-creators! Each of us is called to deal with our life's menu in creative, not destructive, ways.

Our creativity needs to extend both to the micro and the macro dimensions of life. By micro I refer to the ways we deal creatively with our inner issues and the ways we creatively manage all our relationships with family members, friends, professional associates, and casual acquaintances. In short, by micro I refer to all those people whom we encounter in our daily lives.

By macro I refer to the ways in which we nurture our relationships with Earth, with peoples of other cultures, other nations, other races, and other religions. In short, by macro I refer to all those relationships in which we are involved as world citizens and as planetary people.

## Reflection ∽ Transmitters of Divine radiance

*In the beginning was the Word.... (John 1:1)*

At every moment since that beginning, the Word has been uttered. At the present moment the Word is being spoken throughout the Universe. This Word vibrates within and radiates out from every creature. As such, this radiance can be seen as the primary language of the Universe.

The creative Word was spoken and our Universe flared forth into existence some billions of years ago. Let the heavens with its hundred billion galaxies be glad and rejoice. There is no separation here. There is an incarnation (a "flesh-making") of the Divine within the Universe. It is the marriage of the infinite and the finite, and because of this union the Universe is radiant with the Divine presence.

The creative Word was spoken and our beautiful Earth formed out of stardust some four and a half billion years ago. Over time Earth gave birth to its oceans, mountains, forests, prairies, and living creatures of all kinds. Let the ocean and what fills it resound! Let the prairies be joyful and all that lives in them! Let all living creatures exult! No separation here, rather the incarnation of the Divine within Earth. It is the marriage of the infinite and the finite. Earth is radiant with the Divine presence.

The Divine Word was spoken and we humans appeared within Earth's community of life. Let humanity with its awesome diversity of races, cultures, philosophies and religions rejoice. Let humanity with all of its creative achievements in arts and crafts, agriculture and literature, in science and technology be glad. No separation here, rather the incarnation of the Divine with humankind. It is the marriage of the infinite and the finite. All of us are radiant with the Divine presence.

Again the creative Word was uttered approximately 2000 years ago in the city of David to a young woman who gave birth to her first born son and laid him in a manger because there was no room for them in the inn. He was a light that shone in the darkness, and the darkness could not overcome it. His birth gave birth to glad tidings of peace. No separation here, rather the incarnation of the Divine within Jesus of Nazareth. It is the marriage of the infinite and the finite. The child was radiant with the Divine presence, and today those of us who follow in the way pointed out by him are bathed in that same light and celebrate its radiating out of each of us.

Mystics throughout time and in all religious traditions have said the same thing, namely, that we do not have to search for God as if God is hidden from us. The Divine Word is spoken within and radiates out of the Universe and its Earth. It is spoken within and radiates out of Jesus and out of each one of us at this very moment.

# *Reflection* ◌ *The Cosmic Christ*

*He is the image of the invisible God, the firstborn of all*
*creation; for in him all things in heaven and on earth were*
*created.... All things have been created through him and for*
*him. (Colossians 1:15-17)*

This text from the Letter to the Colossians is read in Catholic churches on the Feast of Christ the King. We modern Americans, however,
have a bit of a problem with monarchies. We fought a war of independence to get out from under the foot of the English king. There is
still a king in Belgium, a queen in Denmark, a prince in Monaco, and a
king in Saudi Arabia, but they seem irrelevant to our lives, if not quite
outdated.

So it is difficult for us modern believers to go a long distance
down the road of fully appreciating Christ as King. We do not want
to abandon the image of Christ as a powerful leader and savior, but
I wonder if there is a more modern image to which we can begin to
relate as people of faith? The reading above from the letter to the Colossians provides us with such a Christ. It speaks about "all creation"
and mentions "all things" a number of times. It is an ancient hymn to
the "Cosmic Christ."

All things...like everything that has existed over the 13.7 billion year unfolding of God's Universe. All things...like the estimated
hundred billion galaxies, each containing on the average some hundred million stars. All things...like the 300,000 species of plants and
1.5 million species of animals. All things...from Earth's oldest rocks
in Greenland to the youngest pushing up along the volcanic rifts on
the ocean floor. All things...including all the humans who have ever
existed, exist now, and will exist in the future.

The Universe is the foundational revelation and sacrament. It is the sole place where humans can experience grace. It is performing its mission to show forth the Divine. As Jesus the Christ housed the Divine presence and loving, so too the Universe houses that same presence and loving. As Jesus the Christ in his own unique way embodied and revealed the mystery of God, so too the Universe in its own unique way embodies and reveals the mystery of God. As members of that Universe we too, in our own unique way, embody and reveal the Divine mystery.

# V

# *INTERFACE*

*A*n interface is a place of heightened energy and deep creativity. Consider the interfaces where the Divine and the human meet, where a woman and a man encounter each other, where the outer world touches the inner world, where light and darkness dance together at dawn and dusk, and where the ocean washes up onto the land.

Beginning in the previous century, spirituality entered into a serious interfacing with modern psychology and in that process has been significantly enriched. Our spirituality on the individual and inter-personal levels has become more enlightened and less superficial, more creative and less destructive. We have arrived at a deeper appreciation of and respect for the mystery of being human. This interface with psychology, with which we humans have learned to feel comfortable, continues today.

In recent decades spirituality has also been involved in an interface with sociology, as this social science points to our existence on the public and societal levels. There is social sin and social grace. We now know that spirituality manifests itself not only in the "me" but also in the "us." Spirituality is influenced by social structures and also impacts on them. This interfacing has honed our sense of social justice. This interface with sociology is well underway and it promises to bear much fruit for the future of our human community.

A new urgency is pressing in on us as we enter into the third millennium and its twenty-first century. It is the interfacing of spirituality and ecology. This adventure has only recently begun, and we cannot move into any kind of sustainable future for Earth and its human community without its continuance and nurturance.

Earth is the matrix of the human. It surrounds and supports us. It supplies the air we breathe, the water we drink, and the food we eat. It is the context that nurtures our imaginations as well as our artistic and intellectual lives. It activates our innate sense of the Divine Dynamic.

**Can we make our way not as visitors on the planet but as Earthlings?**

Those of us who have lived our lives within the Judeo-Christian tradition have not distinguished ourselves in concern for Earth. Those of us who believe in a Divine compassion that is present and acting in the Universe are often the very ones who are acting in such destructive ways. It isn't just we as individuals who are doing this. The industrial and consumption-driven economic structures that we have fashioned are also very much to blame.

This interfacing of spirituality and ecology focuses our attention on the inter-connectedness and inter-dependence of all the living and non-living systems of the planet. It invites us to move out of our isolation as a species and embrace our responsibilities within the larger community. It summons us out of our patriarchal stance before all of life into a posture of identity and intimacy with it.

Can we perceive that our nobility as humans comes from the quality of our Earth-human relationships? Can we experience our concern for the fate of the planet as a sacred concern? Can we hear the "cry of the poor" increasing in volume as Earth is increasingly diminished? Can we make our way not as visitors on the planet but as Earthlings?

The most recent interfacing that has emerged is that of spirituality and cosmology. I understand cosmology here not in the narrow sense as defined in the dictionary: "a branch of Astronomy that deals with the origin, structure, and space-time relationships of the universe." Rather, I mean cosmology in a more comprehensive sense as the story of the emergence and unfolding of the Universe and the meaning this drama has for us humans.

Earth could not have been without its Sun, and the Sun needed the Milky Way galaxy, and the Milky Way galaxy needed supernova explosions. This series of transformations leads back to the original flaring forth of the Universe. Cosmology's sustained meditation on this process has revealed that we humans have emerged out of the cosmic evolution. We are who we are only because 13.7 billion years of the Universe's unfolding was what it was. Its story is our story. Our drama is part of its great drama. We can celebrate our spirituality only because the Universe's emergence through deep time has carried a spiritual dimension.

The older view of the Cosmos as fixed and finite, with humanity placed at its center, has been replaced by a changing and seemingly infinite Universe. Within this new understanding, we humans have been pushed out of the center, residing as we do on the third of nine planets orbiting a very ordinary star on the long spiral arm of one of some hundred billion galaxies.

This does not mean that humankind is unimportant. After all, we have made our presence felt in creative and destructive ways everywhere on Earth and now even out into our solar system and galaxy. Some of us feel a cosmic loneliness and a diminishment of personal meaning in the light of this new knowledge about our place in the Universe, and we retreat into the older cosmology, hoping for some security. This security, however, is ephemeral. Thankfully, there is another option for us. We can experience ourselves as "billions of years of evolution reflecting upon itself" (Teilhard de Chardin) or as "rock re-arranging itself" (Brian Swimme) or as "articulated stardust" (Elisabet Sahtouris) or as "a threshold where many infinities meet" (John Donohue). We can celebrate the beauty, sacredness, and future potential of the Universe somewhat in the way parents celebrate the beauty, sacredness, and potential of their children. We can experience and celebrate ourselves as children of the Universe. As we and the Universe continue to evolve, we can expect to be gifted with ever new manifestations of the Divine Dynamic.

These are just a few examples of the many invitations and opportunities that await spirituality as it explores its cosmic path. Indeed, the interfacing of spirituality with ecology and cosmology has become a requirement for the adequacy and vitality of our spirituality as it unfolds in this new century.

## *Reflection* ⁓ *Adventures of hope*

> *Do not human beings have a hard service on earth.... I am allotted months of emptiness.... My life is like a breath; my eye will never again see good. (Job 7:1, 3, 7)*

Some people see the glass as half empty, while others see it as half full. Job sees it as worse than half empty. Crushed by the tribulations of his own situation and the tribulations of others, he laments the harshness of life and sees little or no meaning in the portion that has been given to him. It is filled with pain, grief, and desolation. Hope does not appear on his radar screen. Perhaps many of us, with our years of life experience, can remember times when we were able to identify with Job, at least to some extent.

An adventure is a journey filled with hope. No one starts out upon or continues on in an adventure without the hope that it will result in some benefit, some enrichment, some abundance or betterment. There can be no adventure without the presence of hope.

Consider the Universe within which we live out our life adventures. We discover a Universe that from its beginning has been filled with the Divine creative energy. Imagine billions of years of creativity unfolding galaxies, stars, planets, mountains, rivers, prairies, lakes, plants, animals, and us humans. Yes, us humans! That same Creative Energy flows within you and me. It is available to each of us at every moment if we choose to activate it and become co-creators with God. Is this not reason for us to hope?

Consider the Universe that is itself an adventure. Its story is a story of emergings, breakdowns, and breakthroughs. The breakdowns usually result in something new emerging. For example, the forest burns but the following year all kinds of new life appears. Parents disregard their own needs so that the children whom they love may prosper. This is the Divine Dynamic of dying and rising that permeates the Universe and therefore our personal lives. Is this not reason for us to hope?

# Reflection & Restlessness

> *Come to me, all you that are weary and are carrying heavy burdens, and I will give you rest.... For my yoke is easy, and my burden light. (Matthew 11:28, 30)*

What is this "rest" that Jesus promises in this passage from the Gospel of Matthew? Is it the rest of a contented cow chewing its cud out in the pasture or that of a person relaxing in a hammock under a tree sipping lemonade? The rest that Jesus promises is apparently not like either of these, for the text goes on to talk about a "burden." So the promised rest is some sort of burden. It is an unusual kind of rest indeed. What is this burden?

As twenty-first century followers of Jesus, we are called to be about what he was about. He was focused on a world of justice, peace, and love. He preached about this kind of world in his parables and teaching. He also preached about this kind of world by the way he lived his life. In all this, Jesus exhibited restlessness, an urgency that he could not seem to shake, even to the end.

We also, in our words and actions, are invited to live lives that are restless when it comes to helping to bring about justice, peace, and love. The power to do this resides with the restless Spirit. This Spirit can be spoken of as a wind that blows throughout everything and brings about a Universe that is changing, evolving, never satisfied, and always seeking what is new. We need to allow this wind to blow in the corridors of our lives.

Perhaps you have noticed that I have used the word "restless" several times. This is the yoke Jesus promised. To be about justice, peace, and love means that we always feel restless deep inside, that we are never satisfied with the way things are in the world. This dissatisfaction is our burden, but it is easy and light.

We live in a restless Universe. As humans we are shaped to be restless. This is not a condition to get over or something that needs to be cured. Rather, we need to cherish our restlessness. It is a personal invitation from the Universe to be about what it is about. It is also a personal invitation from Jesus to be about what he was about.

And so to be at peace does not necessarily mean that we feel an inner calm and quiet. To be at peace can also mean that we experience the restless wind. To be at peace can mean being restless our entire lives, not only in our early and middle years but even in our later years. It is a burden that we disciples of Jesus are eager to carry, a yoke we are willing to wear.

# Reflection ✐ All about relationships

*For I desire steadfast love and not sacrifice. (Hosea 6:6)*

There are numerous references to sacrifice in the Hebrew Scriptures. In the time of Abraham, human sacrifice seemed to be a tolerated practice, as evidenced by Abraham's willingness to sacrifice his son Isaac.

In the time of Jesus, the sacrifice of animals was prevalent in the Temple rituals. As an offering for the redemption of their first-born sons, the poor offered a pair of turtledoves or a pair of young pigeons. In the Gospel the parents of Jesus made this sacrificial offering when they brought him to the Temple to present him to God.

The offering of a sacrifice is not something unfamiliar to people of faith in modern times. Some of us are into sacrifice in small ways, for example, when we give up some small pleasures during Lent. Others of us are into sacrifice in big ways, such as parents who sacrifice many of their legitimate needs so that their children might enjoy more of life's blessings.

Let us turn our attention from sacrifice to love, for love is what is desired by God, not sacrifice. In our Christian tradition, the word "love" does not refer to the warm and gushy feelings that we associate with romance. It refers to the entering into and nurturing of authentic life-giving relationships. Who is my neighbor? With whom am I interdependent? With whom do I have mutuality? With whom do I have reciprocity? With whom am I in relationship?

In the Hebrew Scriptures, relationships are generally with members of one's own tribe, one's own people, and include only those who are ritually clean. In the Christian Scriptures, relationships also are with outcasts, the oppressed, and all those who are ritually unclean. In this twenty-first century, with our awareness that we are part of a Universe that is billions of years old, our relational consciousness has expanded exponentially. Our relationships are now as large as the Universe.

In a radical way, each of us is in relationship with all that has happened over deep time. Within the unfolding of the Universe, every reality is in relationship with every other reality and with the Universe itself. It is the interrelatedness of the whole of the Universe that is fundamental.

In the thirteenth century, Hildegard of Bingen wrote the following: "Everything that is in the heavens, on the Earth, and under the Earth is penetrated with connectedness, penetrated with relatedness." A present-day Vietnamese monk, Thich Nhat Hanh, speaks about "interbeing." Another way of saying this is that I am because you are.

## *Reflection ∽ Cosmic feeding*

> *Then Jesus took the loaves, and when he had given thanks, he distributed them to those who were seated; so also the fish, as much as they wanted. (John 6:11)*

In this reading from the Gospel of John, we hear how Jesus, when faced with a large hungry crowd, fed all the people and after everyone had eaten there was much left over.

We live in a society that cherishes the individual. In many ways this is a good thing. We value each person and our individual rights. Our education system seeks to nurture the innate talents of each student. However, we also live in a society that promotes "individualism," and this is not so good. Individualism is an attitude that is so focused on the needs of the individual that it tends to overlook and devalue the needs of the community. Individual rights trump communal rights. The rugged individual becomes society's role model.

Our God certainly cares passionately for each individual. Remember the Scripture passage about how not even one sparrow falls to the ground without God knowing about it. Our passage from the Gospel of John, however, points out that the Divine care is all-inclusive and extends to all. Everyone eats. All are nourished. It is a communal feeding.

Our rugged and narrow individualism sometimes blinds us to the fact that we are first and foremost members of a community. We belong to the human community and to the community of life on Earth. In fact, we would never have seen the light of day and would not have endured, developed, and prospered as a human race without the communities to which we belong. As unique as we may be as individuals, we are expressions of a communal reality. We are members of a family, a church, a country, a planet, and a Universe. All of these communities constitute who we are. We can say little or nothing about ourselves apart from them.

## Reflection ∽ Freedom

*Why, O Lord, do you make us stray from your ways and harden our hearts, so that we do not fear you? (Isaiah 63:17)*

Do these words from Isaiah sound familiar to you? Today many cry out to God saying: Why do you allow so much evil to happen, evils such as wars and terrorism, AIDS and cancers, poverty and hunger, hurricanes, earthquakes, and oil spills? Why is life often so hard? Why don't you do something about at least some of these evils? Our cries and prayers go on and on.

In all of this we are dealing with the problem of evil, a problem that has never been completely answered. Two things, at least, can be said. The first is that we need to move away from the dominant image of God as being at a distance up in heaven. We need to embrace instead the image of a God who is not without but within the Universe and therefore within our individual lives. God is not up in the balcony of the theatre, as it were, watching our lives playing out on the stage of life. Rather, God is on the stage with us, knowing, as Scripture says, even if a "sparrow falls to the ground" (Matthew 10:29).

The second thing to be said is that the God who is present and acting within the Universe is a God who values freedom. The Divine respects freedom. The Divine allows Earth to quake, volcanoes to erupt, hurricanes to blow, cells to become cancerous, mosquitoes to bite, and gravity to cause babies to fall out of their cribs. There is no interfering here. God respects the inner dynamics of the whole Universe and allows each thing to be itself and to unfold according to its own nature, its own laws, and its own spontaneities in the context of much chance and randomness.

Loving human parents respect the freedom of their slowly maturing children. With a certain amount of self-restraint they allow their children to discover the contours of their own lives. Parents even go to the extent of allowing their children the freedom and the space in which to make mistakes and get into difficulties while always inviting them into greater maturity.

In a similar manner, God does not manipulate or control us but exercises a self-restraint befitting a Divine love and allows our lives to unfold each at its own pace and in its own particular way. We humans are even given the freedom to make big mistakes like our present day environmental crisis.

It is, therefore, up to us to be co-creators of our own lives within the freedom that is given to us. Sometimes we do this well, with good results. Sometimes we do it poorly, with bad results.

So, if God respects freedom and does not intervene, the question arises: What does God do? At least two things can be said. First,

God fills the Universe with a creative energy. That energy has been present since the beginning and has been unfolding over cosmic time. Second, God is always holding out before us the possibility of something better. God is always presenting us with many possibilities for our lives, including the possibility of freely transforming this present moment and therefore all future moments.

## *Reflection* ⁓ *Gifts of Divine love*

*See what love the Father has given us, that we should be called children of God. (1 John 3:1)*

How do we experience the Divine love?

This question was asked within a group in which I was participating, and the answers emerged quickly in the group's sharing. One man said that he experienced God loving him through the love of his wife. A woman said she knew God loved her because her children loved her. A young adult said that she experienced God's love through one of her teachers at school who has given her some extra help outside of class.

All of these are inspired answers. They all point out an important truth: namely, that God's love doesn't descend somehow mysteriously from on high but comes to us in and through our life experiences. The wife's love for her husband carried the Divine love for him. The children's love for their mother was the vehicle of the Divine love for her. The teacher's love for that young adult was the vehicle of Divine love for her. In other words, Divine love is embedded within human love.

My contribution to the discussion was to suggest that Divine love comes to us not only through our fellow humans but also through all the other-than-human elements in the Universe. Take a deep breathe,

I said to them. Be aware of the billions of molecules of air entering your lungs at this very moment. Those molecules are also the vehicle of Divine love for you. I went on to invite them into a meditation on the water that they drank earlier in the day and how most of the chemical reactions in their bodies depend upon that water. That water is also a vehicle of Divine love.

God is a giver of gifts, and the Divine love is present within each of those gifts.

## Reflection ∾ Second-half humility

> *Two men went up to the temple to pray, one a Pharisee and the other a tax collector. (Luke 18:10)*

How often we have heard this parable from the Gospel of Luke about the proud Pharisee who proclaims that he is definitely not like others and the tax collector who humbly whispers his radical need for God. I ask myself if there might be a new way, a non-traditional way, to understand this parable. And so I am suggesting that the Pharisee might represent the first half of our lives and the tax collector the second half.

Consider the first half of life. The one-year-old in the high chair throws the spoon on the floor and the mother returns it to the plate. The baby throws it down again and the mother replaces it again. The baby throws it down again and the mother replaces it again…and again…and again. We might conclude that the baby is playing a game, and we would be correct. It is a very serious and necessary game. The baby, like our proud Pharisee friend, is proclaiming that she or he is not like others, not even like the mother, but is a distinct and unique person.

Consider the child who scores a goal in the soccer match or

gets a hit in the Little League game and shouts with pride. Consider the young couple at the baptism of their first child who, with pride, hold their baby up for all in the church to admire. In these examples we can see our friend the proud Pharisee acting, and rightly so.

This is the way it is in the first half of life, and this is the way it needs to be. It is a time for expressing our uniqueness, for being proud of our accomplishments, for making our mark in the world, and for being, to some extent, like the Pharisee.

Now let us turn to the second half of life. Consider the adult in mid-life who begins to nurture old friendships and look for new ones. Consider the adult who finally realizes that to be fully human is to be connected, to be in relationships, and not to be a rugged individual. There is a humility emerging here. It is something like the humility of our friend the tax collector.

Let us look at the older adult who begins to realize that there is more to life than making one's mark in the world, achieving success in one's career, and seeing one's kids through to college. She or he feels the need to submit to the deeper meanings of things, to be connected to what is ultimate and cosmic, and to search for a deep inner place. There is another kind of humility emerging here: a willingness to be led rather than to lead. It is something like the humility of the tax collector.

All of us are being led, from the day we are born, into a new consciousness. It is an awareness of our dependence on the rays of sun falling on Earth and making things green, on the gravitational pull of the moon causing the tides, on the bacteria in the soils and in our own bodies that regulate so many biological processes, on clean air for our lungs and clean water in our mother's wombs for our babies floating there.

Because of this new consciousness, humility is emerging within humankind.

# *Reflection* ~ *The cosmic paradox*

*You are dust and to dust you shall return. (Genesis 3:19)*

All of us can tell the Garden of Eden story because we have heard it so many times. It is the story of God placing the woman and the man in a garden, in a paradise that contained all that they would need to satisfy their human needs. Not content with what God had provided, they violated God's command and thereby brought eventual death upon themselves. In this story the woman and the man, not God, are the cause of death.

There is, however, another part of that same Garden story where we are told that we humans are made out of the dust of the Earth. Dust is a perishable substance, and therefore as creatures of that dust we were never intended to avoid death and decay. It appears that the Creator of that dust does indeed intend that we should experience death.

This understanding is reinforced by the findings of modern science. It has been determined that our Sun, each second of its existence, burns up and transforms four million tons of itself into light, a small amount of which falls upon Earth. Without the Sun's "dying" there would be no life on Earth.

Consider that rocks, when exposed to sun and wind and rain over time, erode and send their minerals into the soils in which we grow our food. In their eroding, the rocks "die" so we might eat our mineral rich food and live with enhanced health. Without that erosion there would be no you and no me.

It seems quite clear that dying and rising are built into the very fabric of the Universe and therefore how our lives work as children of that Universe. We die to a safe life within our mother's womb so that we can rise to a less safe but more exciting life outside. We die to the innocence of childhood so that we can rise to the challenges and excitement of adolescence. We die to the freedom of the single life so that we can rise to the companionship of family life. Parents die to their own legitimate needs so that their children can have a better life. Sooner or later, we humans all die to this life to enter another one. All of this dying and rising—our Sun, the rocks, ourselves—are activating a deep dimension of God's Universe.

Dying is necessary for rising. This is the cosmic paradox.

# VI

# THE COSMIC BANQUET

ℭ

Here is an invitation from the Universe: "You are cordially invited to attend a banquet. Bring only the fullness of who you are. Come ready to celebrate, to eat, and to be food for others." The banquet is a celebration of existence.

The challenge for us today is to know how to enter into this celebratory dimension of the Universe. Primordial peoples apparently knew how to do it. Present day indigenous peoples clearly know how to do it. Why is it so hard for us?

In order to celebrate on this level, at least two things are required. First, we need to see what is actually there before us at the banquet. It is a matter of perception. We need to sense the beauty and the terror as well as the interconnectedness within the Universe. Can we hear the wind among the trees, ever murmuring and ever sighing? Can we allow the river to flow not just *by* us but *through* us? Can we enter into inter-subjective relationships with other life forms? Can we look into the eyes of wild animals and other humans and be overwhelmed by the mystery and depth there? Can we do all these things and respond by saying "awesome" or "marvelous"?

Second, what is required of us to join this banquet is to bring the fullness of who we are as humans to the celebration. This may be easy for the galaxies, the Sun, the rocks, and all the other life forms— what else have they got to do? It is not so easy for us. What is the nature of our uniqueness? How to access our withins? How to arrive at soul? There is no how-to-do book. Those who know and love us can help. There are some helpful guidelines in our sacred scriptures. In the final analysis, however, each of us has to work it out for herself or himself. It can be said that our sadness and confusion is the measure of our running from this task, and our joy and zest for life is the measure of our embracing it.

The banquet table is set with many lovely things. We didn't set the table but we belong at it. We are invited to eat and to drink to our hearts' satisfaction. We are invited to take what we need from the galaxies, the Sun, the rocks, and all the life forms including the humans. We are invited to take what we need for our lives and our souls. Everything and everyone at the celebration is food for us, is gift and grace for us. How blessed we are.

**Our joy and zest for life is the measure of our embracing it.**

At the banquet, we too are invited to be food. We too are part of this cosmological sacrifice. Others have a right to partake of us and nourish themselves from our lives. As one who comes out of the Christian tradition, I wonder if perhaps this is what Jesus of Nazareth had in mind when he said: "This is my body. Take and eat." All of us are among the lovely things on the cosmic banquet table.

To respond to the Universe's invitation requires that we be fully present at the celebration and give our enthusiastic Yes to existence, to life, and to Ultimate Mystery within whose embrace the banquet is taking place.

# Reflection ❧ Come to the feast

*Quickly, bring out a robe—the best one—and put it on him;
put a ring on his finger and sandals on his feet. And get the
fattened calf and kill it, and let us eat and celebrate....*
*(Luke 15:22-23)*

Taking some poetic license and reading between the lines of this text
from the Gospel of Luke, I want to tell the parable of the Prodigal Son
in words that I find meaningful.

The son has been behaving rather badly. He attaches himself to
a Gentile, a move that was a disgrace for a Jew at that time. He works
at feeding the swine, an occupation forbidden by the Law. He longs to
eat what the pigs eat. In desiring this, according to the religious consciousness of the time, his defilement is now complete. After much
reflection on his misery, the son decides to return home. He works
hard at putting together a list of his wrong doings, a list that he will
present to his father and then beg for forgiveness. It is a long list.

Upon seeing his son coming up the road, the father, with tears
flowing, rushes out, hugs him, and kisses him. His lost sheep has returned. His lost precious coin has been found. The son is quite be-
wildered and thrown off balance by this unexpected reception. He
drops onto his knees, reaches into his pocket for his list, pulls it out,
and haltingly begins his well-rehearsed confession. He begs forgiveness for sin number one on his list and then sin number two. He is
just about to begin with sin number three when the father interrupts
and says: "Stop! Enough! That is an impressive list that you have prepared. I am aware of all that went into its preparation, but I am not
interested in your list. What I am interested in is having a banquet to
celebrate your return."

Then the father told his servants: "Put the best robe on him.

Place a ring on his finger and sandals on his feet. Bring in the musicians. Get the word out to his friends. Prepare the fatted calf. We are going to have a banquet."

I have always wondered whether or not the son enjoyed the banquet or was he miserable. If he kept clutching his list of transgressions, he probably did not have a very good time. If he was able to let go of his precious list and focus on the joy and love of his father and his friends, he probably had a ball.

What about you and me? Are we aware of the banquet that God is providing for us? It is a banquet of justice, peace, and love. It is a banquet of life, of clean air to fill our lungs and clean water to quench our thirst, and nourishing food to nurture our vitality.

What about you and me? Are we enjoying ourselves at the banquet? We can enjoy it only if we are aware of God's unconditional love for each one of us. It is a love given to us regardless of what we have written on our lists.

# Reflection ᴄᴑ Being good food

> *Surely goodness and mercy shall follow me all the days of my life. (Psalm 23:6)*

Our most immediate experience of God's goodness is the Universe… the galaxies, the stars, our solar system, our Earth with its ocean, rivers, and lakes; its mountains, deserts, and prairies; its plant life, animal life, and its human life. Yes, its human life! You and I are part of the Divine goodness. This needs to be proclaimed in these modern times.

According to my dictionary, the *goodness* of something can refer to the nutritious and flavorful part. As part of God's goodness, then, we are called to be nutritious and flavorful so that others can taste and see God in their experiences of us.

So, how do we become more nutritious and flavorful? I offer one way to you today. It is the way of "respect." We need to develop the virtue of respect. The English word comes from two Latin words that when put together mean "to look again." Respect is not one of our national virtues. We are a people who drive a thousand miles or more to get to the Grand Canyon, spend a short time there, and then drive on looking for something else to see. We are not experienced at looking again, and again, and again.

Our young people say: "Show me respect." By this they mean: Look at me again and again and again. Don't stop at my surface. See who I really am. See my beauty, my dignity, and my uniqueness.

Years ago when the European ancestors of many of us arrived in the Americas and encountered the native peoples, they looked at them but were unable to look with respect. They were unable to look again and again and again so as to see the beauty, nobility, and mystery of the Native Americans. Instead they enslaved and killed them.

Years ago I took my seven-year-old niece and eight-year-old nephew to see a science fiction film. Whenever there was some special effect in the film, they would turn to me, raise their little fists, and say "awesome" and "excellent." Can we look upon the Universe with everything and everyone that it contains, and be overwhelmed by the beauty, nobility, and mystery there before us? Can we look with respect and say "awesome" and "excellent"? If we can, we will be nutritious and flavorful food for all the others seated at the cosmic banquet.

# Reflection ✐ The banquet of life

*One of the Pharisees asked Jesus to eat with him, and he went into the Pharisee's house and took his place at the table. (Luke 7:36)*

As we read through the gospel stories we discover that many of them, like this one from Luke, take place in the context of sitting down at a table with others and eating.

Life itself is a table at which a meal is served. All life forms are invited to come and dine. All the species are there at the table: some 5,000 species of bacteria; 65,000 species of molds and algae; 10,000 species of fungus; 300,000 species of plants; 50,000 species of worms; 800,000 of insects; 6,000 of reptiles; 7,000 of birds; and 4,500 of mammals. Such is the diversity of life at the banquet: all are life forms that are interconnected and interrelated; all are constitutive of the communion of life on Earth.

We humans, of course, are also privileged to be at the banquet. We are in communion with all the other life forms at the table. We are invited to sit there and to take what we need for our nourishment. We are also invited to be food for all the others at the table. They depend on us to be pro-life in their regard and not destroy their habitats and drive them into extinction.

We can't be pro-life unless we are pro-banquet.

# *Reflection ✑ Great cloud of witnesses*

*Therefore, since we are surrounded by so great a cloud of witnesses, let us also lay aside every weight and the sin that clings so closely, and let us run with perseverance the race that is set before us. (Hebrews 12:1)*

The author of the Letter to the Hebrews is encouraging and exhorting the people to persevere in the face of many difficulties, perhaps even persecution and death, because they are surrounded by a "great cloud of witnesses." In other words, they can find strength in the lives of those around them and those who have gone before them. They can draw upon the courage, faith, hope, and love of that great cloud. We can do the same.

On the level of our own personal lives, let us consider the example of the many people we know who have dealt successfully with the challenges and difficulties of a relationship. Let us focus on the example of those who have struggled through some difficult economic situation or who have engaged with their medical diagnosis in a creative manner. We are surrounded by such a great cloud of witnesses. May their witness nourish us and ease our discouragement and faint heartedness in the face of our many personal difficulties.

On the international level, so many of us feel helpless to do anything about all the wars and violence in the world. Let us focus our attention on the millions of people who are committed to peace making. By and large, their efforts go unreported in the media. They are to be found in every country…countries such as Iraq, Afghanistan, Iran, Israel, the Palestinian Territories, Sudan, and the U.S.A. We are surrounded by such a great cloud of witnesses. Their witness can nourish us and free us from our burden of powerlessness and helplessness in the face of so much violence in our world.

On the planetary level, so many of us are numbed by the shear magnitude of the environmental crisis. What difference can our little bit of recycling make? What we need is to become aware of the planet-wide movement that has emerged in recent years. It has been estimated that there are some one hundred thousand groups and organizations that are concerned about and dedicated to justice for Earth with its human community. This movement has emerged from the bottom up and not from the top down. It is truly a cloud of witnesses.

The Letter to the Hebrews, written two thousand years ago, has relevance for us today. Perhaps we can expand our traditional understanding of the "communion of saints" to include this "great cloud of witnesses" that exists in our twenty-first century. It is a cloud that surrounds us at this very moment. Can you feel its presence? Can you taste its nourishment?

# Reflection ∽ Home

*For the Son of Man came to seek out and to save the lost.*
*(Luke 19:10)*

Are we lost? Where is our true home? According to the traditional story, our original true home was the Garden of Eden, where life was bliss with no work, no pain, and no stress. We lost our way in that garden and were condemned to a state of wandering and homelessness.

Perhaps you realize that this teaching no longer satisfies because it devalues life here on Earth and devalues Earth itself. It suggests that Earth does not have a spiritual dimension and that it is no longer a garden that can nourish our bodies, imaginations, and spirits.

The fact is that Earth carries not only the stuff of our bodies but also the dimensions of our minds and spirits. Separated from Earth, we humans are an abstraction. Our lives spring from the heart of matter. Matter matters. Earth is the nurturing context of all that constitutes our humanity.

We are Earthlings and Earth is where we sit at the table of the Cosmic banquet. Earth is God's designated place for us to be nourished by the Divine Dynamic. Earth is where the Spirit is at work making everything holy…including us. And so Earth indeed remains a garden. It is not a place of exile. It is the only place we have for working out our "Yes" to life and our "Yes" to God. Let us be at home in this sacred place.

## *Reflection* ↷ *Nutrition*

> *But when the king came in to see the guests, he noticed a man who was not wearing a wedding robe. (Matthew 22:11)*

Each one of us at some time has been invited to a feast. Perhaps it was a graduation banquet or a fund-raising dinner or a wedding reception. I remember a wedding feast. The table was set with such detail and beauty that I truly felt welcomed and blessed to be there. In the middle of the table was a vase of beautiful lilies. In front of my chair was a card with my name artistically written on it. My plate with its silverware sparkled in the light. There was a glass for water, a tall thin glass for white wine, and a shorter wide glass for red wine.

Let us focus our attention on the banquet of life. Each one of us began feasting at this banquet from the first moment we were conceived in our mother's womb. We nourished ourselves on the food she ate, the water she drank, and the air she breathed. We have sat at the table of life throughout our lives where we have feasted to our heart's delight on the many lovely items on that table. We have feasted on the abundance provided by the other-than-human aspects of Earth: its Sun, air, water, soil, and the food it produces. We have nourished ourselves on its fowls, fish, and many animals.

We have also feasted on the abundance provided by the human aspect of Earth: our friends, relatives, teachers, and mentors, as well as peoples of other lands, cultures, and religions. We have nourished ourselves on their thoughts, dreams, hopes, and successes. We have fed on the challenges that they have presented to us as well as on their faith, hope, and especially their love. Not only have we accepted the invitation to the banquet but we have been eating voraciously from its menu.

However, we too are among the lovely items listed on the banquet menu. We are part of the abundance that is provided there. The others at the feast have a right to feed themselves on our lives; on our actions, thoughts and dreams; on the challenges that we present to them; on our faith, hope, and especially our love.

That unfortunate person in the Gospel story did not have a proper wedding garment. Perhaps the garment is meant to be symbolic of his inner disposition. Perhaps he wanted to sit there but was unwilling to be one of the lovely items on the table of which the others might partake. Perhaps he was willing to take from the others but was unwilling to give of himself to the others. Blessed are we who have accepted the invitation. Blessed are we who have the proper inner dispositions.

# Reflection 〜 The acceptable sacrifice

*Take your son Isaac, your only son Isaac, whom you love,*
*and go to the land of Moriah, and offer him there as a burnt*
*offering on one of the mountains that I shall show you.*
*(Genesis 22:2)*

Cultural historians tell us that many ancient peoples practiced human sacrifice. It seems that the ancient Celtic people did so in Europe and the Inca people did so in the Americas. The value of human sacrifice appears to have been embedded in the religious consciousness of those ancient times.

We have here this story from Genesis of Abraham being willing to kill his son Isaac for religious reasons. Surely God is not asking this sacrifice of me, Abraham says to himself. Surely God is not asking the unspeakable, the unimaginable, namely, that I turn away from my destiny to have many progeny. Yet it seems that there is a place within Abraham's religious consciousness that allows for the killing of his son.

Evolution takes place within human consciousness in general and human religious consciousness in particular. Let us move from Abraham some seven thousand years ago to the time of Jesus, some two thousand years ago. There has been an evolutionary advance in religious consciousness. Human sacrifice has been abandoned. It is no longer acceptable. The sacrifice of animals, however, continues to be practiced.

We watch as another evolutionary advance in religious consciousness occurs within Jesus. For him, the acceptable sacrifice now has nothing to do with offering animals to God. It is now about offering service to the neighbor: "I was hungry and you gave me food. I was thirsty and you gave me drink. I was a stranger and you welcomed me.

I was naked and you clothed me. I was sick and you visited me. I was in prison and you came to me" (Matthew 25:35-36).

Here we see the outlines of the new acceptable sacrifice. To serve the members of our families…this is the acceptable sacrifice. To serve our friends, associates, and co-workers…this is the acceptable sacrifice. To serve all those people suffering from war and terror, from poverty and hunger, from natural disasters and from ecological diminishment and destruction…this is the acceptable sacrifice. To serve the air, the water, the soil, and all the other creatures upon which we depend for our very existence and upon which Earth depends for its vitality…this is the acceptable sacrifice.

# VII

# ECO-JUSTICE

*[ornament]*

Do you remember the time when a college diploma guaranteed a good job or the time when one could work in the sun without worrying about skin cancer caused by a hole in Earth's ozone layer? Do you remember the time when parents expected that their children would enjoy a better standard of living than they the parents experienced or a time when one could eat fruits and vegetables without being concerned about toxic pesticides? Do you remember the time when global warming and the possibility of a nuclear exchange were not ever present realities? It is none of these times anymore. They have all passed.

The way we humans have organized our societies and economies have not created more employment, lessened poverty, or made us feel more secure. They have, however, slowly and steadily changed the chemistry of our planet, altered its bio-systems, and widened the gap between the human rich and the human poor. The future of Earth has been mortgaged. Life for the human and other-than-human communities of our planet has been diminished, some say beyond recall, and this process continues.

It is time to abandon the illusion that the environment is not central to the long-term economic health and the well-being of all of Earth's citizens. Injustice for the human and destruction of Earth's ecosystems are not two separate injustices. They are one. Hidden within economic poverty today are ecological pathologies. We cannot have healthy humans on a sick planet. Our economic systems can no longer disregard the ways Earth works. Continuing in our illusion is not good for any of us and it is especially hard on the poor and marginalized among us.

It is time for all of us to embrace the reality of our cosmic inter-connectedness. Native Americans tell us about the sacred circle and hoop. The Buddhist tradition speaks of everything being dependent on everything else for its existence. Christian mystics teach us that we cannot fully be ourselves without being in communion with all that exists. Even our scientists now speak about the Universe as being a single energy event, a cosmic communion in which everything in the Universe is present to everything else in the Universe. Lasting justice for Earth and for its humans is only possible within this sacred communion.

**It is time for all of us to embrace the reality of our cosmic inter-connectedness.**

It is time to move out of that consciousness which perceives things in terms of separateness and dualisms. We need to end the worldview that structures reality into superior and inferior, dominant and subordinate. We must stop seeing the human over the rest of the natural world, men over women, First World over Third World, one race and religion over another. Therein is to be found the roots of all the injustices we suffer today. The fundamental conversion required is to see all as interdependent partners sharing in one Earth-human community.

It is time to build a human society that is more truly human and that is radically participative in the dynamics of Earth. There is no longer any time for practitioners of religion and environmentalists to mistrust each other. What is needed is the awareness that the human and the other-than-human are of their very essence connected to each other, both possessing spiritual qualities and basic rights.

Is it possible for those of us who have lost hope to regain it within the cosmic reality of interconnectedness? Is it possible for us to listen to the human poor and the withering Earth and to do justice for both? Is it possible for us, as women and men of faith, to focus our meditation upon the sacred bond that exists between Earth and its humans?

## *Reflection* ✑ *Your ways are not my ways*

*For my thoughts are not your thoughts, nor are your ways my ways. (Isaiah 55:8)*

After the attacks upon the United States on September 11, 2001, a special fund was established to assist the families of those who were killed. Now some are suggesting that a similar fund be established to aid the victims of hurricanes and other natural disasters.

If this fund becomes a reality it will be interesting to see how the money will be allocated. Many will say that those who lost the most should be reimbursed the most. According to this view, the rich and middle class people who have lost the more expensive homes and businesses will receive the larger sums of money while the poor who have lost their cement block shacks and their house trailers will receive smaller amounts. According to this view, those who are best able to bounce back from the catastrophe will receive more money than those who are least able to recover.

Many in our country will look upon the arrangement I have just described and consider it to be fair and just. Can a truly Christian view of things consider that way of allocating the money to be fair and just? Are not the poor, those least able to recover, the ones who have the greater need? Should not a society that claims to be built upon Judeo/Christian values have a special responsibility and preference for the poor and marginalized of society? "For my thoughts are not your thoughts, nor are your ways my ways."

In a familiar Gospel story (Matthew 20:1-16), a landowner goes out at dawn and hires the best workers. These are the ones who are highly motivated and highly skilled, and who have the means to get to the vineyard at an early hour. He goes out again at nine, at noon, and at three in the afternoon to hire more workers. Perhaps these latter workers were not so physically strong or not so skilled or perhaps their family situations and responsibilities kept them from getting to the vineyard at an earlier hour.

We know how the story ends. The landowner pays all the workers the same wage and those who worked the whole day complain that this arrangement is not fair and just. The landowner, however, sees things differently. In his eyes, all of the workers are in need of employment to support their families and so he pays them all the same amount. This financial arrangement is the one that is fair and just for *all* the workers.

A similar scenario is being played out on our withering Earth in this twenty-first century. In our legal system it is only humans who have rights. We do not recognize river rights or tree rights or penguin rights in the Antarctic or polar bear rights in the Arctic. Even to speak this way sounds strange to most of our ears. And so we use, diminish, and even destroy the rivers, the trees, the penguins and the polar bears in the mistaken idea that their existence is only of utilitarian value for us.

In human society in general we live within a hierarchical worldview. It is a posture in which we humans live at the top of the pyramid, with the rivers, trees, penguins, polar bears, and everything else below us. Being at the top, we view everything down below as having no dignity, no truth, no voice, and no rights.

In the Divine view of things, everything that exists has a right to exist, a right to its habitat or place, and a right to continue into the future. In the Divine view of things, everything that exists embodies a spiritual dimension, possesses dignity, contains truth, and has a voice.

## Reflection ✍ A love that leads to justice

*Go therefore, into the main streets, and invite everyone you find to the wedding banquet. (Matthew 22:9)*

The gospels are ancient documents, and like all ancient documents they are sometimes difficult to understand. One thing, however, is crystal clear. The gospels portray Jesus as being totally consumed with and passionate about what he saw as the Reign of God. He preached it, lived it, and died for it.

The Reign of God is the inter-relationship of everyone and everything. It will reach its fullness at some future time, but it is an inter-relationship that is emerging and unfolding in the present time. The Reign of God is a love that leads to justice, a love that seeks a rightful place for everyone and everything. It is a love that includes and embraces and empowers in a particular way the poor, the disenfranchised, and the marginalized.

The Reign of God is sometimes portrayed as an all-inclusive banquet, as in the Gospel passage about those invited to a wedding feast. The first set of guests, those who were originally invited, appear to be respectable, upwardly mobile people who are concerned about their own affairs. They have somewhere else to go and something else to do. And so they don't show up at the feast. It is the street people who end up filling the banquet hall. The feast is enjoyed by those who lack respectability, who do not conceal their hunger for a little food and a little wine, and who have nowhere else to go and nothing else to do.

In the Reign of God there is no preferred treatment for the ruling class, no gold or platinum members of the club. It is a love that shows itself not just in charity but also in justice and is offered to all and empowers all. It is a radical new way of being human. It is the expression of a Christ consciousness. It is a vision of a transformation leading to a radically new future, a future that unfolds out of an all-inclusive love that leads to an all-inclusive justice, a future that results not from power *over* but from power *with*. There is only one justice, and it is offered to all.

# *Reflection* ⟶ *Both mercy and justice*

> *For I was hungry and you gave me food. I was thirsty and you gave me something to drink, I was a stranger and you welcomed me, I was naked and you gave me clothing, I was sick and you took care of me, I was in prison and you visited me. (Matthew 25:35-36)*

If we identify with Jesus and follow in his way, we will engage in the works of mercy as identified in the Gospel of Matthew. We contribute to various organizations involved in disaster relief. We donate to missionary groups who care for the poor in other countries. We make some effort to assist the beggar who approaches us on the street. We work with Habitat for Humanity or volunteer at a food pantry. These works of mercy are important to us because we are serious about loving our dear neighbor.

The importance that we give to these works of mercy, however, needs to be coupled with an emphasis on fixing the unjust social and ecological structures that burden and oppress us humans and our Earth. It is what our Jewish brethren call *"tikkun olam"* ("repairing the fabric of the world").

One such unjust social structure is the ever-widening gap between the rich and the poor in our world. At the beginning of this century, the average income per person in the twenty richest nations was 25,591 dollars a year, but in the poorest nations it was only 211 dollars.

One such unjust ecological structure is the fact that each year in North America we lose some six billion tons of precious topsoil. It blows away or washes away. This loss is mainly due to poor industrial agricultural practices.

How, we ask, can the works of mercy ever make a dent in all of our social and ecological problems? An obvious answer is that they can't. Action for more fundamental change needs to be taken by governments, the World Bank, the United Nations, and especially by the powerful multinational corporations. But this is not enough. We cannot trust these large institutions to do the right thing, unless we also work to hold them accountable.

At the ballot box, we can elect those who are sensitive to the needs of the poor, who understand that we humans are part of the community of life on Earth, and who see clearly that we peoples of the developed world need to be saved from our addiction to consumerism and our extractive economy. We can join or form a group that is studying and taking action on one of the great social issues of the day. Or we can join or form a group that is involved in the greatest of all the issues of our time, stemming the ongoing diminishment and destruction of Earth's life systems.

Another way to put all of this is to say that works of mercy are important because they address the immediate aspect of human misery and that the works of justice are important because they address the deep causes of our planetary and therefore our human suffering.

In this twenty-first century it is becoming clear that the works of mercy alone are an inadequate response to the magnitude of our problems. The works of mercy and the works of justice together have the potential to creatively address and solve these problems.

## Reflection ❧ Stuff and more stuff

*You cannot serve God and wealth. (Luke 16:13)*

We in North America sometimes come close to worshipping our possessions, do we not? For many people, especially younger people, the purpose of life is to make money in order to buy lots of stuff. For many of us, regardless of our age, when we get bored or depressed or can't seem to find needed meaning in life, what do we do? We head out to the mall and buy some more "stuff." This eases our boredom, depression, or lack of meaning—at least until we get the stuff home and if we're lucky for a whole day or two afterwards. Someone has said that our children, by the time they know the twenty-six letters of the alphabet also know twenty-six or more brand names. We cannot serve/worship both the God of Jesus and the god of stuff.

Obviously, we all have a right to consume, to eat, to be clothed, and to be sheltered. We should not, however, exercise these rights apart from our responsibilities for one another and for the integrity and health of planet Earth.

How much food do we have a right to when so many others are malnourished and starving? How many changes of clothing do we have a right to while others go almost naked? How elaborate a home do we have a right to when others are homeless? How much of Earth's riches do we have a right to consume while the life-systems of Earth are under increasing stress? How much do we really need? What are the limits? Throughout human history these have been difficult and complex questions with no easy answers. They are particularly difficult questions at the present time when so many of us feel insecure because of shrinking incomes and skyrocketing healthcare costs. At such a time we tend to turn inward, hunker down in the small rooms within our souls, and focus more on our needs and less on those of others.

But the difficult questions refuse to go away. How much stuff do we really need? What are the limits imposed on us by the teachings of Jesus and by Earth itself?

## *Reflection ◇ Anointed and sacred*

*The spirit of the Lord God is upon me, because the Lord has anointed me; he has sent me to bring good news to the oppressed.... (Isaiah 61:1-2)*

The purpose of anointing in Isaiah's time was to make sacred the person being anointed. What about us Christians? Do we realize that we were anointed with oil and made sacred at our baptism? Some of us were anointed again at our confirmation or ordination, and many of us will be anointed some day with the anointing of the sick.

Apart from these sacramental anointings, do we realize that our very existence, our participation in the Divine Dynamic, means that we are sacred? I have a greeting card that proclaims: Just to be is a blessing and just to live is holy. God looks upon everyone and everything that exists and says that it is very good. This is the primordial, cosmic anointing that permeates the Universe.

After his anointing, Isaiah realized that he was sent to bring good news to the poor. So did Jesus of Nazareth. (Lest we forget, the very word "Christ" means "the anointed one." And so we say Jesus is the Christ using a capital "C.") Yet each of us can also say our first name and follow that name with the words "the christ" with a small "c." For each one of us is also an anointed one.

And if we are anointed ones, then we have been called to the same ministry as Isaiah and Jesus, that is, "to bring good news to the oppressed." This vocation of ours is a heavy responsibility, one that Earth's poor waits for us to fulfill.

## Reflection ⟶ Temples are holy places

> In the temple he found people selling cattle, sheep, and doves, and the money changers seated at their tables....He told those who were selling the doves, "Take those things out of here! Stop making my Father's house a market-place!"
> (John 2:14-16)

Christians believe the Spirit blows in our souls and stirs up the dust there, with the result that things will never be the same again for us. We know that we are temples of that Spirit.

Let us expand this understanding to the entire human community. It too is a temple. The Spirit blows through every country, every race of people, every ethnic group, every religion, and every economic class. Let us expand our knowing even further to include planet Earth. The Spirit hovers over the mountains and the forests, the wetlands and the deserts, the cities and the prairies. It blows within every life form, including bacteria and birds, plants and reptiles, trees and fish, mammals and us humans. Earth is a temple within which the Spirit dwells and is at work. Can we, in our religious imaginations, hear Jesus saying that we need to stop making Earth into a market-place and to stop making everything into a commodity?

For example, health care once was seen as a humanitarian service offered to the sick. Now it has become a product sold mainly to those who can afford to consume it. Health care has been commoditized. Clean water for cooking and drinking was once seen as a universal basic human right to be made available to all at little or no cost. In recent years there has been a trend spreading around the planet where multinational corporations are taking over the management of municipal water supplies, relieving the cash-strapped municipalities of this burden while looking forward to increased profits for themselves by charging ever higher prices for the water. These prices, of course, will be beyond the reach of the poor to pay.

Can we, in our religious imaginations, hear Jesus saying that we need to stop making Earth into a marketplace? Can we hear Jesus saying that we need to stop making Earth into a wasteland and our garden planet into a toxic dump?

Everything and everyone that enjoys the gift of existence is a temple where the Spirit blows. So many of us, however, often approach these temples with our shoes still on, without respect, without reverence, and with little or no awareness that they are holy.

## Reflection ◌ Celebrate the differences

> For if a person with gold rings and in fine clothes comes
> into your assembly, and if a poor person in dirty clothes also
> comes in, and if you take notice of the one wearing the fine
> clothes…have you not made distinctions among yourselves,
> and become judges with evil thoughts? (James 2:2-4)

Let me begin by calling your attention to snowflakes. What is it we all know about snowflakes? They are all different. Scientists have never found two that are exactly alike.

The same is true of everything and everyone in the Universe. Each atom is different from every other atom. Each leaf on a tree is different from every other leaf. Each person, as we well know, is different from every other person. No two are alike. From snowflakes to atoms to leaves to persons, each different individual gives expression to its truth. A scientist friend of mine likes to say that at the heart of the Universe is an outrageous bias for all that is different.

Focusing our attention on humankind, there are differences in gender, race, religion, nationality, ideology, and all the other differences of which we are aware. The problem is that we humans have difficulties with what is different. We are often afraid of or feel threatened by them. And so we tend to rank them. We put them into a hierarchical order so we can exercise some control over them and feel less afraid and less threatened.

Take, for example, the differences between rich and poor. Have we not ranked rich and poor and placed the rich higher up on the ladder than the poor? Have we not thus judged that rich people are better than poor people? In doing this have we not become judges with evil thoughts?

Our society and many of our churches tend to rank men above women, thus judging men to be better than women. In doing this have they not become judges with evil thoughts? Does not our society rank white above color, thus judging white people to be better than persons of darker complexions? In doing this have we not become judges with evil thoughts? Does not our society rank heterosexuals over homosexuals, thus judging heterosexuals to be better than homosexuals? In doing this have we not become judges with evil thoughts? Does not our society rank Christians over Muslims, thus judging Christians to be better than Muslims? In doing this have we not become judges with evil thoughts? This listing goes on.

In the presence of differences, we need to stop all our attempts at ranking. To do this we can take our cue from the Universe. It is a Universe that delights in differences and values them.

# VIII

# DOMAINS OF EMERGENCE

F ive years ago in Poughkeepsie, New York, I was privileged to participate in a ritual at the grave of Pierre Teilhard de Chardin, Jesuit scientist and mystic. During the ritual participants were invited to share the invitations and callings that were washing up on the shores of their souls at that moment. Spontaneously, without any weighing of words, I said that "at the precious age of seventy I am being invited to find my place within Ultimate Mystery, not to rest there but to become a domain of emergence there."

I borrowed the phrase from cosmologist Brian Swimme who speaks of the Universe as always seeking such new domains of emergence. This seeking is a mysterious impulse to transcend the existing order of things. The Universe sought and found new domains of emergence as galaxies and stars within those galaxies unfolded, as Earth was formed and life emerged within its oceans, and as we humans appeared within Earth's community of life with our suspicion that what presently seems impossible might actually come forth in the future.

Looking back over my life, this impulse to transcend the existing order has shown itself as restlessness. As a child and an adult I have delighted in watching thunder and lighting storms and listening to the murmuring and sighing of the wind among the trees. I have experienced myself shuddering before the beauty and the terror of God's Universe.

This restlessness has shaped my life, and the shaping has often occurred at the interface of the personal and the cosmic. This restlessness has most of the time not been problematic for me, although there have been times when I have experienced it as such. Becoming a domain of emergence has not been something to get over. Rather, it has been a gift that has enabled me to sense something more, something that allures and captivates. It has informed many of my life choices. With the passage of the years I have come to cherish this gift. As a Jesuit and follower of Ignatius of Loyola, my restlessness has found warm hospitality in Ignatius' call to be involved in "the greater good."

**Our churches, synagogues, mosques, and temples need to become places where new depths can be accessed and new revelations can emerge.**

Of course I am not the only domain of emergence. All reading these words are called to be domains of emergence. We humans are the mammalian species that has only recently (a mere two million years ago) emerged within Earth's community of life. As such recent arrivals on the scene we are struggling with our precious gift of conscious self-awareness to be a creative presence on Earth.

It is not just individuals who can be domains of emergence. The institutions of society that we create can also be such. For example, our churches, synagogues, mosques, and temples can help us to share this task. They are called to be more than comfortable and safe places for tradition and piety. They need to become places where the Creative Spirit can stir up the dust so that new depths can be accessed and new revelations can emerge.

Our institutions of higher education are also invited to be places dedicated to the emergence and free exploration of ideas that can enhance the human adventure and our presence on Earth. Unfortunately, too many of our schools are busy cultivating what Vandana Shiva calls "monocultures of the mind." What is required at this time of cultural and planetary change is an educational commitment to a creativity that will challenge old paradigms and encourage explorations into new worldviews. We need not fear this kind of exploration. Rather, we can expect an enrichment to result from it.

Our economic structures, especially the ones with addiction to growth and profits, often prevent domains of emergence from happening. For example, they obstruct the creation of more just structures for the poor peoples of the world as well as justice for other life-species. Our present economic system, with its ever-growing gap between the rich and the poor and ever-increasing diminishment of life-systems, is simply not sustainable. A domain of economic emergence calls for a human economy whose bottom line is the nurturance of life and is based on and flows out of Earth's economy.

Shortly before he died, Jesuit Fred Bailey spoke of a "waste of space" on the backs of vertical Jesuit tombstones. He suggested that something personal about the man should be inscribed there. I would like to follow Fred's suggestion and inscribe on the reverse side of Teilhard's tombstone the words: "Here lies a domain of emergence." The powers of God's Universe unfurled within him. Teilhard envisioned humankind in its entirety as being a creative participant in the dynamic unfolding of the Universe. In advance of his time and at a time of worldwide turmoil encompassing two world wars, he spoke passionately of an emerging planetary consciousness.

"The age of nations is past," he wrote. "The task before us now, if we would not perish, is to shake off our ancient prejudices and to build the earth."

# Reflection ⏤ Prophets needed

*And he was transfigured before them, and his face shone like the sun, and his clothes became dazzling white. Suddenly there appeared to them Moses and Elijah talking with him. (Matthew 17:2-3)*

This event chronicled in the Gospel of Matthew happened approximately mid-point in the public life of Jesus. In the first half of his ministry Jesus meets with much success. He draws large crowds and attracts many followers. People, especially the poor and outcast, are eager to hear what he has to say and to receive his healings. Jesus is pleased with how things are going. Perhaps he feels that he is destined for some kind of notoriety and even greatness.

Toward the mid-point of Matthew's Gospel, reading between the lines a bit, it seems that Jesus is growing in the realization that opposition to him is increasing. He is beginning to acknowledge that even his closest disciples are misunderstanding his teachings. He is becoming somewhat disappointed with them and the way his ministry is going. He trusts his calling, but a thought is creeping into his mind and a fear into his soul that perhaps his work will end more in failure than in success.

So he goes up on a mountain to pray, taking three top disciples with him. He is praying about all the changes in his personal situation. Suddenly, through the eyes of the disciples, we see Jesus somehow aware of the presence of the two great Hebrew prophets Moses and Elijah, who are there to remind him that no emergence can take place without some cost.

First is Moses, who himself was destined for greatness. Moses was a champion of the enslaved people and fearless in defending their cause. He trusted his calling, even in the midst of great adversities. Yet

Moses was a failure in the sense that he was not allowed to enter the Promised Land. Moses is present to Jesus and that presence is strength and consolation for the itinerant preacher from Nazareth.

Then there is Elijah, the great prophet of the northern kingdom of Israel. Elijah was known for his courageous deeds and fearless speaking out. His ministry was filled with conflict and opposition. Elijah was often disappointed by the very people he was trying to help. Elijah is present to Jesus and this presence is strength and consolation for the rabbi from Nazareth.

Who are the great prophets present to us today in our twenty-first century? Many would identify women like Dorothy Day, the founder of the Catholic Worker Movement, who lived courageously and non-violently on behalf of the downpressed of society. Another woman prophet is Wangari Maathai, winner of the 2004 Nobel Peace prize, who organized the planting of over ten million trees in Kenya to prevent erosion of the soil and to provide firewood for cooking. Perhaps you have your own names to add to the list of modern women prophets?

Many would identify men like Martin Luther King, Jr., who had a dream of how people might live together in peace and justice and poured out his life's blood that it might be realized. Another might be Al Gore, who has had the courage to remind all of us that if we truly love our grandchildren and great-grandchildren we will make the difficult decisions now regarding the cataclysmic event of global warming. Perhaps you have your own names to add to the list of modern men prophets?

All of these prophets are present to us today, just as Moses and Elijah were present to Jesus. Their presence provides strength and consolation for those of us today who face challenges, the magnitude of which no previous generations ever had to face and who seek to become domains of emergence within these challenges.

# Reflection ∞ The great turning

*Do not be afraid, Mary.... (Luke 1:30)*

I want to write about the cosmic dimension of our Christian faith, about the relationship between Earth and its Sun, and about the shortest day and the longest night of the year. And, like the words of the angel to Mary recorded in Luke, I urge you and myself not to be afraid.

During the last month of each year, the ancient European ancestors of many of us watched as the Sun arose further and further to the south each morning and as the cold and the darkness increased each day. At the time we now call the "winter solstice," they noticed that the Sun stopped its journey south, as if it were deciding whether or not to continue on or start to return back. Fearful that darkness, cold, and death would rule their world forever, these ancient peoples built fires in sacred places and danced around the roaring flames to awaken and bring back the Sun, lest all creation (as they knew it) die in the freezing darkness of an endless winter.

This cosmic event of the Sun halting its journey south has fixed the date of Christmas, for after pausing a few days the Sun does indeed begin its long journey back toward the north—on exactly December 25 each year.

During the winter solstice, we today hear the ancient echoes of the Hebrew people chanting as they light their Hanukkah lamps. We listen to the wind as it carries the prophetic words of promise that a light will come forth. We join the ancient ones in being concerned. Although winter is no longer life threatening for us, as it was for them, we modern people are still in danger that darkness and death will rule over Earth. We continue to wage war and act violently. We threaten the use of nuclear weapons. We are moving the entire planet towards death as we diminish life and resources. Some say that we humans are at the darkest moment of our history. Many of us are fearful and greatly troubled.

The winter solstice, however, tells us that the Sun will continue its great turning toward the north each year, so we need not be afraid. In place of fear, as individuals and as a people, we are invited to become participants in the great turning by becoming domains of emergence in our own lives.

May our violence be turned into understanding and gentleness. May our plundering be turned into reverence and respect. May our greed be turned into sharing. May our consumerism be turned into the joy of simplicity. May our fears be turned into courage.

# Reflection ⁓ Creativity everywhere

*All of them were filled with the Holy Spirit and began to speak in other languages, as the Spirit gave them ability. (Acts 2:4)*

Imagine the creativity and courage that enveloped the disciples of Jesus in this story from the Book of Acts. A moment earlier, they were terrified about the dangers (real and imagined) that might be lurking on the other side of their locked doors.

The first thing we know about what the Spirit does is that the Spirit moves and something new comes forth. In other words, the Spirit is a Creative Spirit. The Creative Spirit was at work at the original flaring forth of our Universe billions of years ago and was also at work when the earliest humans emerged within the community of life here on Earth, some two million years ago.

Often in the past we thought that the Spirit was to be found in what is static, fixed, and unchanging. And so we looked for the presence and activity of the Spirit in such places as unchanging rituals, laws, and traditions. Today we know that we live in an evolving Universe. Now we can discern the Spirit present and acting in places where change is happening and where process, emergence, and unfolding are taking place. These are all places where creativity is obviously at work.

Most people have seen some of those photos taken by the Hubble space telescope. They show the Creative Spirit at work in the birth of stars within far-flung galaxies. Consider how that same Creative Spirit is present and at work within a mother's womb as her baby is foaming into existence.

We have noticed the energy of a child learning how to play a sport, soccer for example. The Creative Spirit is present and at work within that perseverance and determination. We are quite familiar with the trials and errors, the compromising, and the creativity required of two persons who are seeking to build a relationship together. The Creative Spirit is present and at work in all their efforts to nurture their relationship. Some of us personally know about what is required in learning how to grow older gracefully. The Creative Spirit is definitely involved in that learning and that growing.

Contemplate the magnificent outpouring of Divine creativity over the billions of years of cosmic time. That creativity is recorded in the rocks, the trees, and in our human DNA. The Creative Spirit that gave birth to the Universe is present and acting within you and me this day.

How desperately Earth and its human community need the Creative Spirit with its promise of newness. May the Creative Spirit be activated so that the many walls that constrain us might come down and we might become domains of emergence.

# Reflection ∽ Desires are important

*You are my Son, the Beloved, with you I am well pleased.*
*(Mark 1:11)*

As Jesus went down into the warm muddy waters of the Jordan to be baptized and came up into the bright sunlight in this story from the Gospel of Mark, I wonder what he desired. Taking our cue from the whole Gospel story, we can attempt to answer this question.

Like many sons, it appears Jesus wasn't interested in following in his father's footsteps as a carpenter. It seems he desired to be an itinerant teacher, going about all the towns and villages and speaking to the people about God's Reign of justice, peace, and love and speaking especially to the poor and marginalized of his society.

He desired to tell them that God's Reign offers life not death. It is a banquet of grain, wine, milk, and honey for those whose bellies ache. It gives satisfaction to those who are frustrated and disappointed, and promises freedom for those enslaved and imprisoned. Jesus desired to tell that God's Reign is not just some future condition but also a present one, unfolding within each and every one. He desired that his teaching would not return to him empty but would water the Earth, making it increasingly fertile and fruitful. And the Father looked upon this thirty-year-old man from Nazareth with all his desires and said: "I am well pleased."

When I was twelve years old my parents sent me to summer scout camp. Actually, they did not send me as I insisted on going. I remember sitting around campfires at night and staring into the flames, into the part of the flames that seem to have no ending. From deep within me, a desire welled up that my life would have some deep meaning....not bad for a twelve year old kid! Looking back today on that event, I am certain that in that desire I was being allured into my future as a domain of emergence (although I certainly wouldn't have understood that then). Much of my life since then has been an unfolding of that desire. Looking back today on that event, I am certain that the Divine within me looked upon that twelve year old kid with his desire and said:" I am well pleased."

Our desires are important. We need to ponder them, reverence them, and see in what direction they are leading us. What about you? Do you remember some deep desires you had when you were younger? What desires do you find today when you contemplate the landscape of your soul?

## *Reflection ↔ Hearing the word*

> *Welcome with meekness the implanted word that has the power to save your souls. But be doers of the word and not merely hearers.... (James 1:21-22)*

There was a story in the news about a man who killed someone and told the judge that God spoke a word to him telling him to do it. We Christians, as well as those of other faiths, recognize immediately that the word that this man heard was not a word from God. We recognize this because we know that the Divine Word is a life-giving word.

There are many places to which we can go with confidence to encounter the Divine Word being spoken. I call your attention to three of these places.

The first is the truths of our faith, truths that are to be found in our Scriptures and, for Catholics, in the teachings of the Church. We know, however, that the Scriptures can sometimes be misinterpreted. For example, for a long time it was thought that the first two chapters of the Book of Genesis teach scientific facts about the origins of the Universe, but now we know that what they actually teach are spiritual truths about our relationship with God and one another. Sometimes the teachings of the Church can be in error, as well. For example, Galileo was condemned by the Inquisition for saying that the Sun revolved around the Earth and for centuries it was held that slavery was morally acceptable. Generally speaking, however, as adult believers (I stress "adult") we can sit with openness before the Scriptures and the teachings of the Church with the confidence that they will guide us into life-giving actions so that we will become doers and not just hearers of the word.

A second place to which we can go with confidence to hear the life-giving word being spoken is the example of people around us. We can go to the love of spouses for each other, the care that parents give to their children, the tough love that one friend sometimes gives to another, and the actions that individuals and groups are taking to deal with the ecological crisis. Sometimes the people around us are wrong as well. For example, sometimes friends give bad advice to one another. Generally speaking, however, as adults we can sit with openness with the confidence that the people around us will guide us to life-giving actions so that we will become doers and not just hearers of the word.

The third place we can go in order to encounter the Divine Word is the Universe itself. Consider the unimaginable number of different entities, each of which reveals something of the Divine. There are so many different things participating in this great mystery of existence. Consider the dynamics of the Universe and its Earth, dynamics that operate in our individual lives. Sometimes we can misunderstand what the Universe is telling us. For example, there have been cataclysms throughout Earth's history that have made us feel that the physical world is our enemy. Generally speaking, however, we humans can have confidence in all the truths that the Universe makes available to us, truths that will lead us into being doers and not just hearers of the word.

# Reflection ✑ No turning back

> *The whole congregation of the Israelites complained against*
> *Moses and Aaron in the wilderness. The Israelites said to*
> *them, "If only we had died by hand of the Lord in the land of*
> *Egypt, when we sat by the fleshpots and ate our fill of bread,*
> *for you have brought us out into this wilderness to kill this*
> *whole assembly with hunger." (Exodus 16:2-3)*

It seems that the people of the Exodus preferred their former situation of slavery in Egypt, with enough food to eat, rather than their present situation in the desert without enough to fill their bellies. They grumbled. They wanted to turn back.

In Egypt their lives were predictable. Each day's schedule was more or less set in concrete. They knew when to arise, when to work, and when to eat. In this situation they experienced a kind of security. They could depend upon a basic structure for their daily lives and at least know from where their next meal would be forthcoming.

On the other hand, in the desert their lives were far from being set in concrete. Each day unfolded new situations, new problems, new dangers, and new challenges. Gone was the former sense of security. It had been replaced with a sense of vulnerability. Would they perish? Had they made a mistake in leaving Egypt? Was their dream of a Promised Land just that—a dream that was pie-in-the-sky and unreachable?

Life is like that for all of us. We risk the unknown or the little known. We live with a sense of vulnerability. We are courageous and move forward. We are creative. We trust the direction in which we are being led and nurture the hope that a better life lies ahead for us and not behind. We are domains of emergence.

In our twenty-first century there is vulnerability on the societal level where all of the institutions we humans have fashioned over the years are presently undergoing stress. We are challenged as a people to risk facing up to all this institutional stress with creativity and with hope for a better future for all. The temptation is to go back to the old days, to the ways things once were, to perhaps a more innocent and less challenging time. This temptation is an illusion. Life is unfolding. Life is evolving. The way to a more abundant life lies in the future, a future that allures us, however vaguely and obscurely. There can be no turning back.

# IX

# THE PLANETARY HUMAN

*C⌒⊃*

The older cosmology perceived the Universe as being hierarchically ordered, with humans at the top of the pyramid and all the other animals and plants down below with oceans and rocks on the bottom. This worldview contributed mightily to the growth of Western civilization and the nurturance of a much-needed humanism. It possessed also, however, a dark side. It conceived God as above, beyond, and apart from creation, a mainly transcendent deity that occasionally intervened in the Universe. Humankind, being in the image and likeness of the Divine, was also in a state of transcendence or separateness from everything below it on the pyramid.

This worldview created a deep chasm between the human and the other-than human creatures. This chasm had to do with the spiritual. We humans possessed a spiritual dimension while everything below us did not. We humans carried a dimension of the Divine within us, while everything else did not. We alone were in the image and likeness of God. This special status constituted our dignity.

Within this view it was easy for us to see Earth merely as the background against which we carried out our human adventure. It was a radically human-centered view that nurtured a discontinuity between the human community and the other members of Earth's community. It oriented us away from the natural world, a world that had no rights in itself and existed only for human utility. This was the view of a proud human species obsessed with control over everything, a species that understood and experienced itself as being literally the center of the Universe.

The disintegration of this old worldview began in the sixteenth century, when Copernicus displaced Earth as the center of the Universe with his discovery that Earth was in orbit around the Sun. This was not the case according to the religious and secular leaders of his time and place. Then, in the nineteenth century Darwin discovered that we humans were descended from earlier life forms and not the unique creatures of a Divine intervention. In the twentieth century Freud postulated the unconscious, that vast wilderness within us over which we have little or no control. We began to think that perhaps we are not the masters of our fate, and if we are not then what constitutes human dignity?

**We are those beings in which the Universe thinks, reasons, questions, imagines, writes poetry, dances, and sings love songs.**

Modern cosmology, with its growing explanation of an evolving Universe, can provide the basis of a new vision of our human dignity, a dignity arising out of our uniqueness in the Universe. At first glance it seems that we are mere motes living on a tiny planet in orbit around a Sun that is but one sun among some millions of suns in our galaxy, which in turn is but one among some billions of galaxies. From this perspective it seems that we are indeed not that significant.

A closer examination, however, reveals that we are a species of life that looks at itself and wonders why it wonders. We are the only species, as far as we know, that is gifted with this reflective consciousness. It took the dynamics of the Universe billions of years to arrive at the degree of complexity that enabled the emergence of such a consciousness. We are a species whose genetic and cultural endowment carries those eons of creativity. We are what we are because those billion years of cosmic creativity was what it was. Coursing through us is the primordial energy. Indeed, all of this constitutes our dignity.

According to biologist Elisabet Sahtouris, we are "articulated stardust." All of the atoms in our bodies, with the exception of hydrogen, were forged in the furnace of a star that exploded in a supernova several billion years ago. The dust from that explosion came together over time to birth our Sun and our beautiful Earth. Within Earth that stardust formed itself into each of us. According to Jesuit scientist and mystic Teilhard de Chardin, we humans are "billions of years of evolution become conscious of itself." Cosmologist Brian Swimme says that "we are the human form of that power that gave birth to the Universe and guided its evolution." I say that we are those beings (as far as we know) in which the Universe thinks, reasons, questions, imagines, writes poetry, dances, and sings love songs. All of this constitutes our dignity.

There is a desire deep within each of us that is never completely satisfied. It is our desire for relationship, for love. Each of us has an inner-self, a family-self, a friends-and-associates-self, a national-self, a religious-self, an Earth-self, and a Universe-self. Taken together, the sum of all these relationships comprises the total person that each of us is. The nurturing of all these relationships is our life's task. It is our journey into wholeness.

In this twenty-first century, we are invited to embrace our relatedness as Earthlings and as citizens of the Universe. As cosmological people, we exist within a reality greater than ourselves. To the extent that we ignore this reality we become diminished in what makes us fully human. Living creatively as cosmological people enhances our human adventure.

Earth doesn't exist for our exclusive benefit and use, as was assumed in our earlier worldview. Here on Earth, we have discovered ourselves as integral members of the web of life, with responsibilities and privileges flowing out of and proper to our dignity. Our responsibility is to be completely pro-life for the future generations of all the species. Our privilege can be compared to that of the parents of a newborn infant who proudly hold up their baby for the whole world to behold. As planetary people we have the privilege of holding up our beautiful planet Earth and inviting others to stand with us in awe and appreciation.

## *Reflection* ✑ *An all-inclusive salvation*

> *The wilderness and the dry land shall be glad, the desert shall rejoice and blossom; like the crocus it shall blossom abundantly, and rejoice with joy and singing.*
> *(Isaiah 35:1-2)*

These words from the prophet Isaiah are a promise of the Divine blessing of the natural world. It is the blessing of regeneration, of fecundity, of abundance, and of salvation.

Words similar to these words could easily be written by any optimistic twenty-first century ecologist or environmentalist: The rain forests and the fisheries will be restored; the depleted soils will shout for joy as their fertility is enhanced; Earth will return to its former integrity and an Alleluia will be heard throughout the whole Universe.

Moving on from his focus on the natural world, Isaiah focuses next on the human world. "Then the eyes of the blind shall be opened, and the ears of the deaf unstopped; then the lame shall leap like a deer, and the tongue of the speechless sing for joy." (Isaiah 35:5-6) His words are a promise of the Divine blessing of humankind. It too is the blessing of restoration, of healing, of wholeness, in other words, of salvation.

Words similar to these could easily be written by any optimistic twenty-first century social activist: Then will Jews and Palestinians sit down for tea together and Christians and Muslims enter into respectful and serious dialogue; then will the gap between the rich and the poor be narrowed; and then will all of humanity sing songs of peace and reconciliation.

In his focus on both the natural world and the human world, Isaiah speaks of the promise of salvation. I call your attention to the fact that it is not salvation for the one and then for the other, as if they are two separate entities. Rather, it is the promise of salvation for the whole that is Universe, for the whole that is Earth, and for the whole that is Earth's human community.

We moderns tend to separate the natural world from the human world. In fact, we live almost completely in our human world and, generally speaking, we give only an occasional nod to the natural world. But the Divine relates to both the natural world and the human world as one. In fact, they are one. God's love is being poured out into the whole Universe. Where the Divine love is being poured out, there salvation is taking place.

# *Reflection* ☙ *The Divine within*

*Ask a sign from the Lord your God; let it be deep as Sheol or high as heaven.... Therefore the Lord himself will give you a sign. Look, the young woman is with child and shall bear a son, and shall name him Immanuel. (Isaiah 7:10, 14)*

When Isaiah speaks here about a sign that is deep and high, he is speaking out of his ancient understanding of the Universe, about a sign that is a cosmic sign. If Isaiah were speaking today about this sign, he might say that it is as deep as the DNA that guides the foaming into existence of the fetus within the womb and as high as the furthest galaxy at the outermost edge of the Universe.

Isaiah goes on to say that the sign will be named "Immanuel" which means "God is with us." As women and men of faith we take "Immanuel" seriously. We take the idea that "God is with us" literally.

The Divine is within on the macro or comprehensive level. So we can find God in all things in the Universe. We can find God not only in human realities but also in all the other-than-human realities. Everything and everyone that has come into existence within the billions of years of the Universe's unfolding—and that will come forth in the future—reveals and embodies the Divine Dynamic. Another way is to say it is that everything and everyone carries the Divine presence and the love.

God is also present on the micro or personal level, that is, in all the rooms within the mansion that is your precious life and mine. On the first floor of the mansion there are some large rooms. One has a sign on it marked "good times" and another with a sign that says "good health" and another room marked "success" and a fourth room marked "happiness and joy." We often go into these first floor rooms. We like to go into them. We keep the doors into these rooms open all the time. We expect to find the Divine within and loving us when we enter these rooms.

On the second floor of the mansion there are some smaller rooms. One has a sign on it marked "failures" and another room has a sign that says "struggles" and another room with a sign that says "difficulties" and a fourth room marked "misunderstandings." We frequently find ourselves in these second floor rooms, although we don't exactly enjoy going into them. We keep the doors of these rooms closed most of the time. Often we do not expect to find the Divine within and loving us in these rooms.

Up in the attic of the mansion are a few very small rooms. One has a sign marked "suffering" and another designated as "sickness" and another marked "tragedy" and a fourth room with a sign that says "dying." We avoid going up into the attic if at all possible. We keep the rooms locked up there. When we are forced to go up into these rooms, it is often difficult for us to find the Divine within and loving us there.

The truth, however, is that God is within and loving us in all of the rooms of our mansion. As we believe this, so may we live it. The truth is also that God is within and loving in everything that shares existence with us in the Universe. As we believe this, so may we live it.

# Reflection ⟂ People of the rocks

> *He brought Simon to Jesus, who looked at him and said, "You are Simon son of John. You are to be called Cephas" (which is translated as Peter). (John 1:42)*

It is clear from reading the Gospels that some 2000 years ago a small group of followers of Jesus of Nazareth, aflame with his teachings and his Spirit, began to live and proclaim a radically new message of good news for the poor. A fisherman named Simon, nicknamed Peter, which means "rock," occupied a position of responsibility among the followers. Peter wasn't perfect by any means, but he was great. He had lots of love in his heart and allowed that love to unfold. Peter influenced the faith of those early Christians to the point that he was eventually recognized as the leader of the small group, upon which "rock" the believing community was to be built.

We are also people of the rock that is Earth. It has been determined by our scientists that some four and a half billion years ago Earth was a fiery ball of molten rock in the sky in which heavier chemical elements like iron sank into its core while lighter elements floated on its surface, a surface perhaps resembling the lava we observe flowing from present day volcanoes.

Over time Earth cooled, an atmosphere formed, and it began to rain. For thousands of years the waters fell as Earth formed it oceans and shaped its continents. Deep in the ocean during this time chemical processes were giving birth to the awesome mystery of life. At first there were one-celled creatures followed by the multi-celled animals such as jelly fish, worms, fish, insects, green plants, trees, amphibians, reptiles, flowers of all colors, mammals, chimps, and finally the first humans. With the humans there emerged languages and cultures, covered wagons and spacecraft, crayons and computers, songs, dances, poems, prayers, and all of us gathered here on the Earth today.

All that I have just listed has unfolded over time from that fiery ball of molten rock. It is a sacred process. Physically we are children of that molten rock. Its atoms are our atoms. Our bodies are as old as that rock. Spiritually we are also children of that molten rock. For each moment of our existence it is present to us and we are present to it. Our depths and mystery are intimately connected to the depths and mystery of that rock. To understand our own creativity and spiritual dimension we need to understand the creativity and spiritual dimension of that rock. In fact, we are that molten rock, after four and a half billion years, having become conscious of itself.

# Reflection  ∽  People of the clays

> *Then the Lord God formed man from the dust of the ground,*
> *and breathed into his nostrils the breath of life....*
> *(Genesis 2:7)*

According to this famous passage from Genesis, we humans are made from Earth's dust (or clay). This is not a diminution or humiliation. It does not make our species somehow less significant or less noble as some like to say.

Earth's dust is not just some configuration of atoms that doesn't amount to much. It is a material reality, to be sure, but also a spiritual reality. In fact, it is a sacred reality. The Spirit is present and at work in that dust. We can say that Earth's dust or clay embodies the Divine Dynamic.

And so, over time and with the help of sunlight, rain, and some other things, Earth's clay has been very creative. It has been able to become everything and everyone on Earth. Taking a few examples from the gospel stories, clay has formed itself into donkeys, pigeons, camels, dogs, sheep, goats, foxes, fish, snakes, scorpions, birds, pearls, doves, flowers, lilies, trees, grapes, olives, and people. All the humans who have ever lived, our ancestors, Abraham and Sarah, Moses and Miriam, Zechariah and Elizabeth, Joseph and Mary, Jesus, and all of us alive today have come from Earth's clay.

God loves that clay and all that comes from that clay. Our souls are not something disengaged from body, from matter, from the clay. Rather, our souls are totally embedded in the clay. We are invited to embrace the mystery that is the clay, to embrace it forever inside us and inside everything else.

# Reflection ∽ People of the waters

*Strike the rock, and water will come out of it, so that the people may drink. (Exodus 17:3, 6)*

As winter slowly turns toward spring, the waters of the melting snows slowly seeps into the soils. The water fills up the mountain streams and the prairie rivers. Rural farmers and city gardeners alike look forward to spring with its promise of rains and new life.

We are mostly water. As an embryo floating in the water of our mother's womb, each of us was approximately 97% water. Even in our old age, each of us is or will be approximately 60% water. Water is the essence of our vitality. Earth's water is where all life began. Water is more than a symbol of life. Water is life. Water is sacred.

Water seeps into the cracks of rocks. It expands as it freezes, splitting the hardest rocks and leaching out minerals necessary for life. Moving in rivers, water serves to grind rocks down into fine particles of minerals that feed the plants. Water can seep into all things and change them forever. We originated in the ocean and we carry the ocean within us.

Every person who exists has a birthright to clean water. This basic right should be included in our Bill of Rights, but it isn't. We have made water into a commodity, something to be bought and sold like one more "product" to be swallowed up by the black hole of our out-of-control consumerism.

For those of us who are people of faith, water is sacramental. It is an outward sign of the life-giving and loving presence of God. When we thirst and quench our thirst with water we are receiving the gift of life and being loved by the Divine. Water is not just some important stuff. It is a sacred reality.

When we drink some water it is not like pouring gas into an

engine. The gas provides energy for the engine but does not become the engine. On the other hand, the water we drink moves into our blood streams, into our brains, into ourselves. It becomes us. It becomes the sparkle in our eyes and the tears flowing down our cheeks. It becomes our songs, our dances, and our loves. It becomes our sorrows and struggles, our prayers and worship.

We dare not take water for granted. Let us be thankful for it and become a spring of living water ourselves, a spring of living water for our Earth and its community of life…a spring to which others can come and quench their unending thirst.

## *Reflection ⌇ Beatitudes revisited*

*Blessed are the poor in spirit…. Blessed are the meek….*
*Blessed are the peacemakers…. (Matthew 5:3, 5, 9)*

Did this teaching from the Gospel of Matthew make any sense to the people at the time of Jesus? I can imagine some of them, especially the young people, saying to themselves:"Get real! Where are the blessings for us?"They lived in a society where the rich had the strongest voice and the poor little or no voice. It was a society in which the meek were trampled upon. It was a society in which peace was a cruel hope for a people suffering under an oppressive occupation by the hated Romans."Get real! Where are the blessings for us?"

Do the Beatitudes make any more sense in the societies of our time? Our twenty-first century is certainly a time when the rich have the dominant voice in determining what happens, not the poor. It is a time when power is firmly in the hands of dictators, presidents, corporations, definitely not with the meek. And it is a time when peacemakers often seem like little Davids trying to confront the Goliaths of the military and industrial establishments. It is easy for many modern people to dismiss the Beatitudes as some sort of pious and utopian teaching. "Get real! Where are the blessings for us?"

Seen from an ecological perspective, however, the Beatitudes take on surprising significance for us moderns.

From this perspective the poor—not the destitute poor to be sure, but those who have adopted a simple lifestyle—these are the ones who carry hope for our world community whose other members are moving toward or are already trapped in an unhealthy and unsustainable consumerism. Only those who live simply, consume only what is required to live with dignity, and avoid the sin of over-consumption, can lead us out of our profligate ways. Only those who embrace a simple lifestyle can promise a future in which Earth and its human community will exist together in a mutually enhancing manner. Blessed, indeed, are the poor in spirit.

Viewed through an ecological lens, the meek are the ones who offer a sustainable future for all of us. Recall the parable where Jesus is critical of those whose egos move them to take the first places at the banquet table. We humans have become those who assume the places of honor at the banquet of life. But the well-being of our withering Earth can only be realized by moving beyond our human egos. Only if we nurture within ourselves the virtue of meekness, only if we humans assume our proper place within Earth's web of life, will the planetary withering be slowed down and brought to a halt. Blessed, indeed, are the meek.

An ecological worldview also has much to teach us about the importance of being peacemakers. Within Earth's life systems, all living creatures learn to find their proper place, what is called their "ecological niche." In this niche they nourish themselves and raise their offspring. Here they also learn how to be creative within the larger system rather than weaken or destroy it. Recall the parable about the Lilies of the Field. The lilies live within their ecological niche, where they have certain responsibilities and where they enjoy certain blessings. They are not concerned with accumulating stuff and becoming dominant. They are free to be their authentic selves and in this freedom they are beautiful.

We humans need to be like the lilies of the field, free from accumulating stuff and increasing our dominance. We need to be free to deal creatively with all of life's challenges and invitations, free to act in a creative manner with all that is going on today between nations, religions, ideologies, political parties, and other interest groups who share Earth with us. Blessed, indeed, are the peacemakers.

## *Reflection ✍ Vanity of vanities*

> *The land of a rich man produced abundantly. And he thought to himself, "What shall I do, for I have no place to store my crops?" Then he said, "I will do this: I will pull down my barns and build larger ones...." But God said to him, "You fool! This very night your life is being demanded of you. And the things you have prepared, whose will they be?" (Luke 12:16-20)*

In this parable from the Gospel, Jesus does not criticize the man because he is rich but because he cannot see beyond his riches, beyond his huge stock of grain. The man's self-image and self-worth is tied up in his wealth. He has an excessive attachment to and love of his possessions, a love bordering on a worshipping of them.

All of us are caught up to some extent in a fascination with and love of acquiring things. I have a niece who, in a moment of cynical reflection during her mid-thirties, said: "You are born, you buy, you die."

Who among us, in a time of feeling bored with life, has not gone off to buy something only to discover that the happiness resulting from that purchase was transitory? In our own way, each of us is like the man in the Gospel parable. Our self-image is caught up in the accumulation of things. It is a self-image that sooner or later always turns out to be ephemeral.

When a reporter asked President George W. Bush why he wasn't asking ordinary citizens to sacrifice more for the war efforts in Afghanistan and Iraq, his answer was that they should sacrifice by going out and buying more things. His answer was satisfactory to a large number of people who viewed the solution to many problems in terms of filling our national barns and silos by purchasing and accumulating more and more stuff.

This behavior is indeed "the vanity of vanities." (Ecclesiastes 1:2) An escape from such vanity is provided for us in ancient wisdoms and in the findings of modern science. Both of these sources tell us that using more and more stuff is not the way to go. They tell us that to be authentically human we need to move out of the use mentality and begin to experience ourselves primarily as people in relationship. In God's Universe, to be is to be in relationship. Nothing stands as an island unto itself. Such a posture is indeed "the vanity of vanities."

# Reflection ↬ Flame meditation

*All things came into being through him, and without him not one thing came into being. What has come into being in him was life, and the life was the light of all people. (John 1:3)*

As I end this book of reflections on the Divine Dynamic, the relationships between humans, the Earth, and the creative power of the Universe, I ask you to light a candle with me as we focus our attention on its light, its flame.

Let the flame evoke within us the memory of the primordial

creation event some billions of years ago, when out of a fertile noth-ingness a great fire billowed out in all directions. Our Universe was born then. God's Word was spoken there. The Divine Artist was at work there. It was an art show to surpass all art shows. You and I were being loved there.

Let the flame with its heat evoke within us the memory of the intense heat of a star that exploded some several billion years ago, giving birth to our sun and from the scraps of that birth our beautiful blue-green Earth. You and I were being loved there.

Let the flame evoke within us a memory of Earth some four and a half billion years ago, when it was a lava-like fiery ball of molten rock in the sky that over time formed a crust upon which we stand today. You and I were being loved there.

Let the flame evoke within us a memory of the earliest humans, who sat around their own fires and gazed into their own flickering flames while their shadows danced behind them on the cave walls. You and I were being loved there.

Let the flame evoke within us the memory of that burning bush before which Moses stood, with his shoes off and his knees shaking, experiencing the Divine Dynamic calling him to the cutting edges of his life. You and I were being loved there.

Let the flame evoke within us the memory of those fires on the hillsides and lakesides of Galilee, around which the rabbi Jesus sat instructing his disciples. You and I were being loved there.

Let the flame evoke within us memories of our parents and grandparents who sat before their fireplaces, lanterns, and candles while they dreamed great dreams for their children. You and I were being loved there.

Let the flame make us aware of the fire that burns deep within us, a fire that embraces us with all our successes and failures, hopes and fears, joys and anxieties, good moments and not-so-good ones. It is a Divine love that invites us to move confidently and creatively into our unimaginable future, the future of our Earth, and the future of the whole Universe.